PERT Study Guide 2020:

PERT Study Guide Book, Test Prep, Practice Questions for Florida

TABLE OF CONTENTS

ABOUT THE PERT EXAM

Congratulations! You've decided to enter the world of higher-education. You're in for a long journey ahead, but you've made an excellent decision. Your study partners at Spire wish you the best of luck in your new career.

The first order of business is to successfully pass the PERT exam. The PERT is an admissions exam used to determine your readiness in a few different areas. Students who take the PERT must be prepared to complete reading, mathematics, and writing sections on the exam.

SCORING

If you want to pass the PERT, you need to know how well you have to perform. Different schools will have different scoring rubrics, but most usually require that you score a certain number in each exam category. Minimum scores are dependent on the schools you apply to, so be sure to check with the admissions office of your school for specific scoring requirements.

EXAM BREAKDOWN

Now that you know the score you need to get, let's talk about the actual PERT exam. Below is a breakdown of the number of questions on the PERT exam:

READING - 20 Questions

WRITING – 300-600 Word Essay

MATHEMATICS – 30 Questions

Please note that the number of questions on the PERT will not be the same for all students. It is an approximation that varies for each individual taking the test.

Now that you know the overall structure of the test, it's time to dig into the information.

Good luck, and let's get started!

READING

Finding the Main Idea

Many of the reading comprehension questions you will encounter on the exam are structured around finding the main idea of a paragraph. The last section on root words was all about finding the main idea of a word – notice a theme developing here?

In this section, you will need to find the main idea of a paragraph. Luckily, that's nice and simple once you know what to look for.

First of all, we're going to re-define a few terms you might think you already know, so don't rush through this part:

Paragraph

A paragraph is a tool for organizing information. It's simply a container for sentences in the same way that a sentence is a container for words. Okay, maybe you knew that already, but you'd be surprised how many professional writers get their minds blown when they realize that almost all books are structured in the same way:

Books are made of chapters, which are made of sections, which are made of paragraphs, which are made of sentences, which are made of words. It's a simple hierarchy, and smack in the center is the humble paragraph. For the purposes of the test, you need to be able to comb through given paragraphs to find two kinds of sentences: topic and detail.

Topic Sentence

A well-written paragraph, which is to say all of the paragraphs that you'll find on the test, contains just one topic. You'll find this in the topic sentence, which is the backbone of the paragraph. The topic sentence tells you what the paragraph is about. All of the other sentences exist solely to support this topic sentence which, more often than not, is the first or last sentence in the paragraph. However, that's not always the case, so use this foolproof method: Ask yourself, "Who or what is this paragraph about?" Then find the sentence that answers your question.

Detail Sentence

Detail sentences exist to support the topic sentence. They do so with all kinds of additional information, such as descriptions, arguments and nuances. An author includes detail sentences to explain why they're writing about the topic in the first place. That is, the detail sentences contain the author's point, which you'll need in order to find the main idea. To easily spot the author's point, just ask yourself, "Why is the author writing about this topic?" Then pay close attention to the detail sentences to pry out their motivations.

Got it? Good. Now, let's do some really easy math: The topic + the author's point = the main idea. Now, let's put that in English: What + Why = Main Idea.

In the Real World

All right, you've got the abstract concepts nailed down. Now, let's get concrete. Imagine a scenario where a friend is explaining the movie Toy Story to you. Also, imagine that she has already picked her jaw up off the floor, because seriously, how have you not seen Toy Story? You should fix that.

She tells you what the movie is about: There are these toys that get lost, and they have a bunch of adventures trying to get back to their owner. Then she tells you why you should see it: It's cute and funny, and it's a classic.

Two sentences: The topic (what the movie is about) and the author's point (why she's telling you about it.) And now you have the main idea: Your friend thinks you should see the movie Toy Story because it's a cute, funny classic about toys having adventures.

Illustrating the Main Idea

Here is a paragraph similar to one you might encounter on the test, followed by the types of questions that you will need to answer:

EXAMPLE 1 – from The Art of Conversation by Catherine Blyth:
"Silence is meaningful. You may imagine that silence says nothing. In fact, in any spoken communication, it plays a repertoire of roles. Just as, mathematically speaking, Earth should be called Sea, since most of the planet is covered in it, so conversation might be renamed silence, as it comprises 40 to 50 percent of an average utterance, excluding pauses for others to talk and the enveloping silence of those paying attention (or not, as the case may be.)"

This one is relatively easy, but let's break it down:

- Who/What is the paragraph about? Silence.
- Why is the author writing about this topic? It is often overlooked, but it's an important part of conversation.
- What is the main idea? Silence is an important part of conversation. Or, put it another way: "Silence is meaningful" - it's the first sentence!

Okay, you've seen the technique in action, so now it's your turn. Read the following paragraphs and determine the topic sentence, the author's main point, and the main idea.

To find the main idea of any piece of writing, remember: The topic + the author's point = the main idea or What + Why = Main Idea

Practice Time!

Let's see what you have learned about finding the main idea and focal points of a passage. Read the following passages below. Search for topic and main idea, and try to determine the focus of each one. Then answer the questions presented after each passage.

Good Luck!

Passage 1

Regardless of your reasons and motivations, if you choose to homeschool your child, there are many factors that must be considered. One of the most hotly debated is that of providing a means of socialization for students. The fear some people have is that students taught at home rather than a traditional school setting do not get the social interaction with peers that regular students do. There are many ways children can socialize and interact with others their age:

Group field trips- there are groups and certain organizations that help host group fields trips. Homeschooled students can also get together with other homeschool students or their friends and peers who are in public or private schools and attend field trips together. These trips also can serve as credit for the homeschooled student's class work- historical monuments can count as history credit and a report written about what was seen can count as an English assignment; they also get the benefit of having time with their friends and peers.

Community service- there is always an opportunity to get involved in the community and these are perfect opportunities to interact with others. Students can get together to work on a project or can work on their own and work alongside others who are volunteering at the same location. It helps get your child interacting with others and can also help to instill valuable life lessons at the same time.

Scouts, clubs, and programs- there are many organizations that offer the opportunity for students to work, learn, and grow alongside each other. Boy Scouts and Girl Scouts offer a chance for students to interact with their peers while developing their own life skills. The 4-H Program also offers a unique opportunity for homeschooled students to get life experiences and interaction; some 4-H clubs are set up especially for homeschooled students.

Co-op Groups- these exist to help families organize group events with fellow homeschool students. Group projects and study sessions are just some of the options that are available. Group study sessions can also be prepared to practice for things such as SAT testing, Finally, homeschooled families can take advantage of co-op groups to help set up study sessions and events for students. These are just a handful of simple ways home school families can answer society's question about how students can be socially active and interact with students their own age. Following the simple tips and taking a stab at any others that may be out there is a great way to meet your child's socialization needs while providing them with peace and protection and the education you want them to receive.

1. Which sentence best states the main idea of this passage?
A)   Homeschool children lack any good socialization and peer interaction.
B)   There are many ways children can socialize and interact with others their age.
C)   Children who are homeschooled lack major social skills.
D)   None of the above.

Answer: B. Throughout the piece, the author talks about how homeschooled children can still find ways to socialize and interact with their peers.

2. Which of the following is not a way homeschooled students can interact with their peers that was discussed in this passage?
    A) Join a club or social group
    B) Volunteer in the local community
    C) Go on field trips
    D) They all are ways homeschooled students can meet peers

Answer: D. All three of those methods of socialization were talked about in detail within the passage. Every one of them had several examples and explanations given as to why they were effective means of getting homeschooled students around their peer group.

Passage 2
The world around us is filled with the weird and usual. When we think of freaks of nature we usually bring to mind images of massive rabbits, six legged cows, and two headed dogs.
However, the usual species and 'freaks of nature' also spill over into the plant world. Usual plants offer a unique look at plant biology gone haywire. From excessive size to usual smell, these freaky plants are real and can be found today -if you know where to look.

Although more than 90% of plant types have leaves, used for photosynthesis, there are some scenes and varieties of plants that do not. The most common of these are members of the mushroom family that are parasitic in nature. They feed off the decaying material of plants or suck nutrients from healthy living plants. One such parasitic plant truly earns the title of usual. It is the Rafflesia arnoldii. This plant bears a bloom that can grow more than three feet in diameter. The flower smells like rotting flesh and has a hole in the center big and deep enough to hold up to six quarts of water. To top off the list of usual traits, this plant has no stems, roots, or leaves, a true freak of nature.

Flowers can range in size from a fraction of the size of the plant, to more than 80% of the plant itself. Flowers serve as the reproductive part of the plant and is responsible for producing seeds to further the next batch of plants to be grown according to that plant's individual biology. One of the plants that show this wide range in plant size is the group of plants known as Amorphophallus. Closely related to the peace lily, these plants have a similar flower. Found in the subtropics, more than 200 different species and varieties have been identified. One of these species, Amorphophallus titanum, has a bloom that is several times larger than the plant itself; the blooms can get so large on some plants that they can exceed the height and width of a grown adult. Truly amazing what plant biology is capable of.
Many species of trees and flowering plants are quite old. The methuselah trees of the desert and the great redwood giants of the forests are just two well-known examples of ancient species still living. But perhaps the most ancient of all is a plant that was believed to have been long extinct. Until 1944, the plant known as Wollemia nobilis was known only by the fossil remains. Then living plants of this

type were discovered in remote tropical areas. The bark is unique as it is a deep chocolate color and looks like it is comprised of many tiny bubbles. This is not tiny plant either as some specimens have been records at heights of over 120 feet. It is believed that there are maybe only 100 of these plants left in the wild.

Plant biology is an interesting branch of science. A great deal can be learned about nature and the world around us by studying plants. This field of study gets even more interesting when the unusual plant species that populate the world are taken into consideration. Every corner of the world hold surprises. Who knows, there may still be colossal giants hidden away in remote rainforests and miniscule plants hiding in the crevasse of a mountain side just waiting to be discovered.

1. Which point do the details in this passage support?
   - A) Plants have many different features
   - B) All plants are basically the same in their biologic makeup
   - C) Plants must share similar characteristics in order to be plants
   - D) None of the above

Answer: A. All the details in this passage talk about how plants are different from each other yet still are considered to be plants- some have leaves whole others do not and some are big while others are little. Plants can look vastly different from each other and still belong to the plant family.

2. What did the author want the reader to get out of reading this passage?
   - A) That plants are amazing and very diverse in the way they look
   - B) Not all plants look like the flowers and trees we are familiar with
   - C) Some plants are very old and some are still waiting to be discovered
   - D) All of the above

Answer: D. All of these points are correct because they are all mentioned within the passage and discussed and described in detail.

How did you do? If you still need some help figuring out the main idea and topics of passages like these, keep practicing!

Detail Questions

Reading passages and identifying important details is an important part of the critical reading process. Detail questions ask the reader to recall specific information about the main idea. These details are often found in the examples given in the passage and can contain anecdotes, data or descriptions, among other details.

For example, if you are reading a passage about certain types of dogs, you may be asked to remember details about breeds, sizes and coat color and patterns. As you read through the following passages, make sure you take note of numbers, figures and the details given about the topic. Chances are you will need to remember some of these.

There is a wealth of information, facts, pieces of data and several details that can be presented within any passage you read. The key to uncovering the main idea and understanding the details presented is to take your time and read through everything contained in the passage. Consider each example and figure presented. Think about how they relate to the main idea, how they support the focus, and how those details add to the information and value of the passage.

Read the following news article and answer the following questions.

Passage 1

Police of Chicago are searching for two men who under investigation for charges of impersonating cops. The men stopped a person on the city's Northwest Side. In a bit of an ironic twist, the two fake cops ended up pulling over an actual Chicago cop.

Officials say the officer who is in his 40's was finishing his shift and on his way home when he was pulled over. It was in Chicago's Avondale neighborhood just after midnight when the officer had a white SUV pull up behind him and flash its lights. The officer saw the signaling, said the SUV looked like a police issued undercover vehicle, and pulled over. According to reports, one of the two men exited of the unmarked car, wearing normal civilian clothes. The man approached the cop, who was still wearing his bullet proof vest, and said he was with the Chicago police.
The officer said that the civilian clothes and lack of standard police issued items alerted him that something was wrong and he challenged them on that statement. The two men ran back to the unmarked car and sped off and disappeared into the dark streets. The Chicago police describe the suspects as two Hispanic men in their early to mid 20s who are both around 6 feet tall and around 150 pounds. Anyone with tips should call the Chicago Police Department.

Questions:

1.What is the passage above mostly about?

A) Problems with the Chicago Police Department

B) A news report about people pretending to be police officers

C) Chicago Police are cracking down on crime

D) None of the above

Answer: B There is a sentence that specifically states that the report is about two men who were pretending to be Chicago Police officers.

2.According to the passage, what details were given about the incident?

A) Civilian clothes and lack of standard police issued items made the cop suspicious

B) The event occurred in Chicago's Avondale neighborhood just after midnight

C) The two men who posed as Chicago Police officers were of Hispanic decent

D) The police officer was in his 40's and the two fake cops were in their 20's

E) All of the above

Answer: E All of these details were mentioned throughout the news report.

3. All of the following are things we know about the real officer in this story except:

A) His Age

B) His duty status at the time

C) How long he's been with the Chicago Police

D) We know all these things

Answer: C Nowhere in the article is it mentioned how long the real officer has been serving with the Chicago Police Department.

Remember:

There is a wealth of information, many facts, countless pieces of data, and a lot of details that can be presented within any passage that you read. The key to uncovering the main idea and understanding all the details that are presented is to take your time and read through everything contained in the passage. Read everything and take the time to consider every example and every figure presented and see how it relates to the main idea and how to supports the focus and how those details add to the information and value of the passage you are reading.

Reading passages and picking out these important details is a big part of being an effective reader. Practice makes perfect and the more you read the more you analyze and the more you work on it the better you will get and the more you will be able to pull from any article, blog, story, or report you read!

Understanding Question Stems

In addition to careful reading of the passages (including marking up the text for topic and concluding sentences, transitional words and key terms), you must also be able to identify what is being asked of you in each of the questions. Recognition of the task in each question can be easily accomplished if you are familiar with the question stems, or the most commonly phrased wording that will be associated with each type of question on the test. Keep reading for an explanation of each question type, along with sample stems, and suggested approaches for tackling them.

Main Idea

Questions asking you to identify the main idea expect that you will be able to determine the overall point of the passage (often called the thesis), NOT secondary details or supporting points. Attempting to put the main idea into your own words after reading WITHOUT looking at the text again is a very helpful strategy in answering this type of question. If you can sum up the author's main point in your own words, then you will find it very easy to find the right "match" amongst the answers provided for you. Alternately, the main idea may often be found in the opening or concluding paragraphs, two common places where an author may introduce a topic and his perspective about said topic, or he summarize the main points.

Here are some common ways this type of question is asked:
- The main idea for this paragraph...
- The central point of the passage...
- A possible title for the passage...
- The author's primary point...

Supporting Details

Supporting details are those that back up the main ideas presented in the passage. These can include examples, clarifying explanations, or elaborations of basic ideas presented earlier in the reading. Supporting details are directly stated in the passage, so you must rely on your careful reading to guide you to the correct answer. Answers may not be stated in the original language of the passage, but the basic ideas will be the same.

Here are some common ways this type of question is asked:
- The passage states...
- The author says...
- According to what you read...

Inference

Inferences are those ideas which can be gleaned from the suggestions that may be implied in other statements made by the author. They are never explicitly stated, but we understand that they are true from "reading between the lines". The answers to inferences questions, therefore, are assumptions, and cannot be found from direct statements in the text. You will have to rely on your ability to logically deduce conclusions from your careful reading. More than one answer may sound correct, but only one is. Make sure that, whichever answer you choose, you can find statements in the text support that idea. If you cannot do that, then that choice is likely not the right answer.

Here are some common ways this type of question is asked:
- The passage implies...
- The author suggests...

- The reader could logically conclude that...
- The reader would be correct in assuming that...

Tone/Attitude

Some questions will ask you about the author's tone or attitude. A good place to start with this type of question is to consider whether the passage is positive, negative or neutral. Does the author seem angry? Maybe sad? Or torn between two points of view? The language that an author uses can be very telling about his tone and attitude. Is the author critical? Praiseworthy? Disappointed? Even if you find some finer details of passage difficult to understand, the tone and attitude are often fairly easy to identify. Look for adjectives and statements that reveal the author's opinion, rather than facts, and this will help you know his tone or attitude.

Here are some common ways this type of question is asked:

- The tone of the passage is...
- The attitude of the author is...
- The writer's overall feeling...

Style

Style refers to a writer's "way with words". Most seasoned writers have a well-developed and easily recognizable style. but often the topic of a written work can dictate style. If the topic is serious the language will likely be more formal. Works for academic settings may be heavy with the jargon of that discipline. Personal reflections can be rife with imagery, while instructional manuals will use simple and straightforward language. Identifying style is not difficult; simply pay attention to the words used (simple or fancy?), the sentence structure (simple or compound-complex?), as well as the overall structure of the piece (stream of consciousness or 5-paragraph essay?). You must answer these questions in order to determine the style of the passage.

Here are some common ways this type of question is asked:

- The overall writing style used in the passage...
- The author's style is...
- The organizational style of the passage is...

Pattern of Organization

Pattern of organization questions want you to consider how the writing of a piece was developed. What features did the writer utilize to make his point? Did he include personal anecdotes? Data or statistics? Quotes from authorities on the topic? These are all modes of organizing a passage that help the writer support his claims and provide a logical focus for the work.

Here are some common ways this type of question is asked:

- The author proves a point through...
- In the passage, the author uses...
- Throughout the passage, the author seems to rely on...

Purpose and Attitude

Questions asking about purpose and attitude require you to consider why the author took the time to write. The authors motivations are directly behind the purpose of the piece. What question did he wish to answer? What cause did he want to show support for? What action did he wish to persuade you to take? Identifying these reasons for writing will reveal the purpose and attitude of the passage.

Here are some common ways this type of question is asked:

- The purpose of the passage is...
- The author's intent for writing the passage is...
- The attitude the author displays is...

Fact/Opinion

There will be some questions on the test that will ask you whether a statement is a fact or an opinion. Without being able to fact-check, how will you do this? A rule of thumb would be that opinions reflect only the thoughts, feelings or ideas of the writer, whereas facts are verifiable as true or false, regardless of one's feelings. if a writer cites a statistic about the environmental effects of oil drilling on migratory mammals in the Pacific Northwest, then that is verifiable and can be considered factual. If, however, the writer claims that oil drilling in the Pacific Northwest United States is bad and should be stopped, then that is his opinion. He may at some point provide examples of why this is so, but that viewpoint is based on his thoughts and feelings about oil drilling, and can only be considered opinion.

Here are some common ways this type of question is asked:

- Which statement is a fact rather than an opinion?
- This statement is meant to be...
- An example of fact is when the author says...
- An example of opinion is when the author states that...

Eliminating Wrong Answers

An author often writes with an intended purpose in mind, and they will support their main idea with examples, facts, data and stories that help the overall meaning of their written text to be clear. You may be asked a question regarding one of these details or examples or about the overall theme or main idea of the passage. These types of questions require you to read the passage carefully for meaning and to look at all the supporting details used. However, it's also important to learn how to identify incorrect answer choices and eliminate them right away. This will help you narrow down the answer choices that are likely to be correct. Here's how you do it:

Strategies for Answering Specific Detail Questions:

• Identify the key words in the question that help you find details and examples that will help answer the question.

• Make mental notes as you read the passage about how words are used and the phrases that are repeated. Also look for the overall meaning of each paragraph and passage.

• Some questions will pull words or phrases from the passage and use them in the question. In this case, look through the passage and find those words or phrases and make sure they are being used the same way in both the passage and the question. Many questions will change the meaning of these to make the question wrong or confuse the reader.

• Some questions will ask you to determine if a particular statement about the passage or topic of the passage is true. In this case, look over the paragraphs and find the overall theme or idea of the passage. Compare your theme or idea to the statement in the question.

Now it is your turn to try it out and see how you do. Read the following passages and answer the questions, making sure you eliminate the wrong answers as you look for the right one. There will be three passages for you to read and several questions about each one- there will be one right answer and at least three wrong answers you will need to eliminate as you read. Good luck!

Passage 1
Online game play has become standard for many video games. While it allows your kids the opportunity to play with other fans of their favorite games, it also brings with it new risks and dangers. By being proactive and staying active with their children, parents can ensure video games remain safe and fun for their kids.

Parents need to stay current on several things- video game ratings, content clues, and their kid's use and involvement. The ratings on video games can help parents know what is and is not acceptable content for their kids.

Parents also need to keep an eye on the content of the games once the game play starts- peek in now and then to make sure there is nothing surprising lurking in a game you thought was fine. Also, parents need to monitor how often their kids are playing the games, the time spent playing, and how much time is spent thinking about the game. Balance is critical to make sure video game use remains fun and safe.

Make sure you keep communication lines open with your kids. They need to know that they can come to you with questions, concerns, or problems. They need to feel safe talking to you and not be fearful that you will be made or angry with them. When your child comes to you with a problem do not brush it off- be sure to give it the attention it deserves and make sure they know you are glad they are coming to you.

Questions:
1. Parents can ensure video games remain safe and fun for their kids by doing what?
A) Be proactive with your decisions
B) Be active and involved with your kids
C) Be willing to let your kids do what they want
D) A and B
E) B and C

Answer: D. Both A and B are correct since they were mentioned in one of the first sentences in the opening paragraph of the passage

2. What do parents need to do to keep their kids safe while playing video games?
A) Stay current on trends and news
B) Monitor kid's game activities
C) Communicate with kids often
D) All of the above
E) None of the above

Answer: D. All of these are things mentioned in the passage when it talks about the things people can do to keep their kids safe while playing games and playing online.

Remember reading all the paragraphs is a great way to get the overall idea of the passage. Also every paragraph of a passage should be discussing a different example or point that ties back to the main idea of the passage and helps further demonstrate the main idea.

Passage 2
Kids of all ages have long loved drawing and many kids will draw on anything and everything they can get their hands on. Thy will draw on paper, the floor, their clothes, themselves, and of course the walls! Many parents turn to the tried and true chalkboards for their kids' play room, or play area.

However, chalk can be messy, is harder to clean up, and some kids just don't like the light powdery look of their chalk artwork. If this is the situation you are in, you will want to consider dry-erase paint as the most practical solution to your dilemma. Years ago when dry erase was something you saw only in school or in office buildings, it was hard to come by if you wanted that option at home.

Dry erase easels and boards were cumbersome, bulky, heavy, and expensive. However, now you can actually get specially formulated dry erase paint that you can use on your walls to turn them into massive dry erase boards! Dry-erase has low odor, low-chemical content, and is suitable for a range of surfaces such as wood, brick, concrete, and many others.

Why stifle their creativity when you can unleash it and let them create, design, and explore the wonders of their own imagination? Many companies carry dry erase paint so you can transform your child's bedroom or play room into the best place in the world. Whether you want to give them a section of the wall, one entire wall, or all the wall space they can reach, this one little addition can help make it easy for you to give them ample room to be creative.

Image the smile on your child's face to see a daily message written to them on the wall when they wake up or when they come home from school. Send gentle reminders about chores and homework or use the dry erase space for a fun approach to the nightly homework sessions. Be creative and you will never run out of uses for the Create Pain dry erase paint.

Questions:

1. What are some reasons mentioned in the passage for why dry erase walls are a good choice for a kid's room?
   A) Easy to clean and helps kids be creative
   B) Safe and less chemicals
   C) Are able to be used for every day needs
   D) All of the above

   Answer: D All of the answers are correct and are mentioned in the passage- they are not all mentioned in one paragraph but they are mentioned throughout the passage and all tie back to the idea of dry erase being a good option for your kid's room.

2. Only a few companies carry dry erase paint to be used on walls, which makes it hard to find and use for kid's room designs. Is this statement *True* or *False*?

   Answer: False. In the passage it does mention getting dry erase paint from companies but says that many companies carry it. So this means it is fairly easy to find and use and is a good choice for kid's rooms.

Passage 3
We hear a lot of talk about recycling nowadays. We recycle glass, plastic, newspaper, and there are countless ways to reuse everyday items to keep them out of the landfill for a little longer. An equally important, but not as discussed method of recycling is scrap metal recycling. You may be wondering why it is such a big deal and what good metal recycling can make- well, let's take a look.

One of the biggest impacts this form of recycling has is it conserves raw resources and eliminated the carbon footprint for many metal production facilities. The Institute of Scrap Recycling Industries (ISRI) states that in 2010, more than $64billion was added to the United States economy; all of it came from the recycling, reuse, and production of new products from recycled metals. All of this metal scrap would otherwise end up in the landfills or in the environment and that much more raw material would have to be mined and refined and produced from scratch to make new tools, machines, and products. Scrap metal recycling is a very important aspect of conservation and pollution reduction.

In addition to the economic impact from profits of reusing scrap metal, the act of metal recycling also generates jobs. The ISRI estimated that in 2008, over 85,000 jobs were supported and made possible in some way thanks to scrap metal recycling. It also helps in trade sand exports, as it was estimated that over $28 billion and roughly 44 million metric tons of metal was shipped and sold overseas.

Scrap metal recycling comes in many forms. Sometimes it is a junk yard or scrap yard that buys scrap metal and then sells it to manufacturers who can melt it down, refine it, and use it to make new

products and materials. Or it could be the neighborhood scrap collector who visits yard sales and stops by your trash pile to pick up that old dishwasher or microwave you threw out.
There are also community sponsored recycling programs where cans are collected and turned in for cash, or programs such as the electronics recycling and business incentives for recycling scrap metal left over from production or building projects.

It is easy to see the benefits and importance of scrap metal recycling. Whether it is some materials left over after a home renovation project, tin cans your kids have collected, or the last remaining pieces to that old junk car you scraped, recycling the scrap metal can do a world of good and have a lasting impact on the environment, economy, and your local community. So do your part and be on the lookout for scrap metal to add to your recycling piles.

Questions:

1. The ISRI is a company that oversees scrap metal and recycling practices. True or False?

    True- the ISRI is the Institute of Scrap Recycling Industries and in the passage we see that they offer reports about money earned from scrap metal recycling and also talks about the job market associated with scrap metal recycling.

2. Recycling scrap metal helps the environment by keeping that junk out of landfills. True or False?

    True- the passage talks about recycling and how it is a very important aspect of conservation and pollution reduction.

    Good job- remember to read every passage you are given carefully and don't be afraid to go back and read something again or scan the passage for key words and phrases that show up in the questions.

Inferences and How to Make Them and Use Them
Inference is a mental process by which you reach a conclusion based on specific evidence. Inferences are the stock and trade of detectives examining clues, of doctors diagnosing diseases, and of car mechanics repairing engines. We infer motives, purpose and intentions.

You use inference every day. You interpret actions to be examples of behavioral characteristics, intents or expressions of particular feelings. You infer it is raining when you see someone with an open umbrella. You infer that people are thirsty if they ask for a glass of water. You infer that evidence in a text is authoritative when it is attributed to a scholar in that particular field.

You want to find significance. You listen to remarks and want to make sense of them. What might the speaker mean? Why is he or she saying that? You must go beyond specific remarks to determine underlying significance or broader meaning. When you read that someone cheated on his or her income taxes, you might take that as an example of financial ingenuity, daring or stupidity. You seek purposes and reasons.

Inferences are not random. While they may come about mysteriously with sudden recognition, you usually make inferences very orderly. Inferences may be guesses, but they are educated guesses based on supporting evidence. The evidence requires that you reach a specific conclusion.

Inferences are not achieved with mathematical rigor, and they do not have the certainty obtained with deductive reasoning. Inferences tend to reflect prior knowledge and experience as well as personal beliefs and assumptions. Thus, inferences tend to reflect your stake in a situation or your interests in the outcome. People may reason differently or bring different assumptions or premises to bear. This is why bias is addressed so carefully in our criminal justice system, so defendants are given a fair trial.

Given evidence that polychlorinated biphenyls (PCB) cause cancer in people and that PCB's are in a particular water system, all reasonable people would reach the conclusion that the water system is dangerous to people. But, given evidence that there is an increase in skin cancer among people who sun bathe, not all people would conclude that sunbathing causes skin cancer. Sun bathing, they might argue, may be coincidental with exposure to other cancer-causing factors.

*Daniel J. Kurland (www.criticalreading.com/inference_process.htm)

Inference Questions

Inference questions ask about ideas that are not directly stated, but rather are implied by the passage. They ask you to draw conclusions based on the information in the passage. Inference questions usually include words like "imply," "infer" or "conclude," or they may ask you what the author "would probably" think or do in a given situation based on what was stated in the passage.

With inference questions, it is important not to go too far beyond the scope of the passage. You are not expected to make any guesses. There is a single correct answer that is a logical, next-step conclusion from what is presented in the passage.

Let's take a look at some sample inference questions. Read through the following passages and use your inference skills to answer the questions. Remember that the inferences you make are not always obvious or directly stated in the passage.

Passage 1

Despite the fact that the practice is illegal in many states, some people set off their own fireworks at home each summer, especially on Independence Day. Most cities have public fireworks displays run by experienced professionals in a controlled environment, but many people still enjoy the thrill of setting off their own fireworks. However, this practice can be dangerous, and many people are injured each year from fireworks-related accidents. Having Independence Day fireworks in your own backyard is not worth the safety risk, especially when public fireworks display are available in most areas.

Questions:

1. The author of this passage would most likely support:
A. The complete legalization of fireworks nationwide
B. The reduction of public fireworks displays
C. More rigorous enforcement of restrictions on home fireworks
D. Promoting home fireworks use

Answer: C.
In the passage, the author takes a negative tone toward home fireworks use, citing the fact that the practice is dangerous, illegal in some areas and unnecessary since many areas have safe public fireworks displays on holidays. Someone who is critical of home fireworks use would support strong enforcement of restrictions on their use.

Passage 2
A man took his car to the mechanic because the engine was overheating. The mechanic opened the hood to inspect the situation. He removed the radiator cap and could see that there was a sufficient amount of coolant in the radiator. He took the car for a drive and also noticed that the engine would overheat at a stoplight, but not on the highway.

Questions:

1. According to the passage, what can you infer about the engine?
A. The engine needs to be replaced
B. The radiator is leaking
C. The engine is operating normally
D. The radiator fan is broken

Answer: D.
Although an overheating engine does indicate an abnormal condition, it does not necessarily indicate a catastrophic failure. Thus, the engine can be repaired instead of replaced. The radiator was full of coolant, so that eliminates the possibility of a leak. When a vehicle is moving, the airflow across the radiator cools the coolant. However, when a vehicle is stationary, the fan is responsible for cooling the coolant. If the fan is not working correctly, this would explain the overheating at a stoplight, but not on the highway.

Passage 3
One man in St. Paul Minnesota is making a difference for people in the community, and his impact was felt stronger than ever this Thanksgiving Holiday. Jeff Ansorge once was in charge of almost 20 staff members and earned $80,000 a year as the head executive chef at a classy downtown Minneapolis restaurant. Only for the very well-off, the restaurant featured items such as a 24-ounce dry aged Porterhouse steak that went for almost $50. However, Jeff gave it all up to and has taken on the job of head cook of a Salvation Army soup kitchen. Where meals would cost $40-$60, now his meals are free.

As head cook he is making salmon, ribs, and stews for those who come to The Salvation Army Eastside Corps Community Center in St. Paul. For the Thanksgiving meal that's Jeff had the traditional meal of turkey with stuffing, along with mashed potatoes and gravy, and even the extras like cranberry sauce and rolls. Even the ambiance was completed with dinner being served on tables covered with white tablecloths and simple decorations. Jeff Ansorge, who is 40, says that it was a spiritual awakening that prompted him make the move to the soup kitchen in October 2012, where he is now making just one-third of his previous salary.

Not only did Jeff bring his culinary skills but his eye for bargain shopping and his ability to make food stretch has allowed the Salvation Army to serve great food and actually save some money in the process. The Salvation Army works along with Second Harvest Heartland food bank and with Jeff's help, they can now get 40-pound cases of mixed poultry for as little as five bucks. Jeff Ansorge also does his best to bring nutritional value to every meal that he serves. He knows that for many who come to the soup kitchen, it may be the only meal they get for the day. He's eliminated desserts and is also working to cut back on the fat and sugars in meals, giving more room for fresh fruits and vegetables and healthy meats.

Questions:

1. Jeff is a caring and compassionate individual who has a deep sense of right and wrong and is likely governed by deeply held beliefs and ideas of mortality and civil duty. True or False?

   Answer: True. Several things mentioned in this passage can lead you to infer this about Jeff- he was raised in the Catholic faith, he works in a soup kitchen, volunteers, gave up a good job to help others, and genuinely seems to care about those who are less fortunate than himself.

2. All people who are well off and making good money dislike people like Jeff who make them look bad. True or False?

   Answer: False. Nowhere in the passage is this hinted to or implied at all.

Remember inferences can be tricky things to master. Practice makes perfect so keep at it!

MATHEMATICS

- Convert among non-negative fractions, decimals and percentages
- Divide the numerator by the denominator
- Moving decimal points to make percentages
- Decimals into fractions by simplifying ratios

Essential to an understanding of fractions, is the concept of division. Whole numbers divided by whole numbers will always result in decimal answers. Continuing that division until a zero remainder will provide the complete decimal representation of the original fraction. A decimal answer less than one is the result for a proper fraction division. The answer greater than one is the result of an improper fraction division, when the numerator is greater than the denominator. This process of division will always allow conversion of fractions into decimals.

Every fraction represents a division problem. The decimal value of any fraction is represented by the numerator, (top value), divided by the denominator (bottom value). Certain combinations, such as $^1/_3$, will result in repeating decimals that will always require rounding in a testing situation.

The fraction $^1/_2$ has a decimal value of 0.5, which is the value of 1 divided by 2. The values of improper fractions such as $^3/_2, ^5/_2,$ or $^7/_2$ (larger numerator than denominator) are determined by dividing as previously stated or more easily by multiplying the numerator by 0.5. So the improper fraction of $^7/_2$ is 7 x 0.5 or 3.5. Often the determination of the unit fraction (1 divided by the denominator) followed by the decimal multiplication is simpler in a testing situation.

The fraction $^3/_5$ has a decimal value of 0.6, which is the value of 3 divided by 5. Alternately, the value of the unit fraction of $^1/_5$ is 0.2 and that unit fraction multiplied by 3 is 0.6. If you know the unit fractions for common fraction values, the test answer selection may be simplified.

When a fraction such as $^5/_7$ is evaluated the quotient of 5 divided by 7 results in a lengthy decimal value of 0.71428…. That extended value will never appear as a multiple-choice test answer selection. Typically, that value will be rounded to either 0.71 or 0.714. Remember that testing instructions say to choose the **best answer**. Your best choice may be a rounded number.

If we look at the fraction $^3/_4$, the division of numerator divided by denominator is 3 divided by 4. Since 4 cannot be divided into 3 evenly, the first division becomes 3.0 divided by 4 which is 0.7 with a remainder of 0.2. When we complete the next step of division, .20 divided by 4 has an answer of 0.05 with a remainder of zero. When the remainder is zero, the division is complete. The completed division answer is 0.75, the correct decimal representation of $^3/_4$.

The next step in the conversion process is the comparatively simple step of converting a decimal to a percentage. The term, "percent", means "per one hundred", which is simply a fraction with 100 in the denominator. Therefore, a decimal can simply be converted to a percentage by moving the decimal point in the correct direction. In the previous example where the answer was 0.75, that ratio is 75/100. Since percentage means "per one hundred", our percentage is 75%.

The remaining part of this process is the conversion of a decimal to a fraction, which completes the cycle and implies that we have a complete repertoire of skills to deal with fractions. The basic way to convert back to a fraction from a decimal is to write the decimal in fraction form. In our previous example, our answer was 75/100. This is the decimal representation of the percentage, and it is a fraction but not in simplest form. To simplify any fraction, we look for common factors in both the numerator and the denominator. If we choose 5 as a common factor 75/100 becomes (15*5)/ (20*5). The common factors can be eliminated in both the numerator and denominator, so the fraction becomes 15/20. While this is a fraction, it is not yet in simplest form, since there are other common factors. The fraction becomes (3*5) / (4*5) which is ¾, the simplified form.

As you read this description, you may have thought that there was a simpler method. In fact, there was a common factor of 25 in both the numerator and denominator at the beginning. This process could have been executed in one step if you saw that 25 was the common factor. If you did not see that, please understand that this process of simplification can be accomplished in several steps if necessary. Whether it is completed in one step or more, as long as the final ratio has no common factors in the numerator and denominator, the simplification process is complete and successful. Most important is that you have completed the process of converting a decimal or percentage into a fraction. Your fraction skill set is on the way to completion. In the next section, the we will continue by adding, subtracting, multiplying and dividing fractions.

M.1.2. Perform arithmetic operations with rational numbers

- Add & subtract
- Like denominators
- Finding common denominators
- Multiply & divide
- Numerators times numerators etc.
- Invert the divisor before multiplying for division
- PEMDAS

Recall that rational numbers or fractions are made up of numerator and a denominator. The top number of the fraction, called the numerator, tells how many of the fractional parts are being represented. The bottom number, called the denominator, tells how many equal parts the whole is divided into. For this reason, fractions with different denominators cannot be added together because different denominators are as different as "apples and oranges". Therefore, when adding (or subtracting) fractions with different denominators, a "common" denominator must be found. In a later section (7. Multiples) there is a review of multiples, but the common denominator is an application of that principle that we will apply here first. In this case, simple geometric models will be used to explain the common denominator principle. Usually this principle is illustrated with circles divide into "pie slices". A simpler and more complete example involves the use of squares or rectangles divided into fractional parts.

Representing fraction parts $^1/_3$ and ¼ will be demonstrated with the following square diagrams. In this case a whole square is the number "1" and the fractional parts will be the slices of the square as follows:

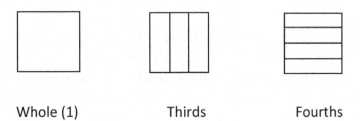

Whole (1)   Thirds   Fourths

If we superimpose the four horizontal slices over the three vertical slices, there are twelve separate parts of the whole as follows:

In the last diagram, any column that represents a third, has four of the twelve small rectangles from the diagram or $^4/_{12}$ as the equivalent fraction.

Similarly, any row of the last diagram that represents a fourth, has three of the twelve small rectangles from the diagram or $^3/_{12}$ as the equivalent fraction. With this modification of the two fractions, both have been modified in the form of a common denominator and the addition of the two fractions can be completed:

$$1/_3 + ¼ = {}^3/_{12} + {}^4/_{12} = {}^7/_{12}$$

Notice that this result is directly analogous to the geometric diagram above. Common denominator fractions need not be simplified with a diagram, but it is a valuable example to explain the principle. The common denominator is required whenever fraction addition or subtraction is required but the denominators different. If the denominators are the same, then the addition or subtraction of numerators is all that is required. If more assistance is needed on how to find common denominators, start by finding the least common multiple which provides the required lowest common denominator for addition. The example below shows the multiples of 3 and 4

Multiples of 3:	3	6	9	<u>12</u>	15	18	21	<u>24</u>	27...
Multiples of 4:	4	8	<u>12</u>	16	20	<u>24</u>	28	32	36 ...

Notice that there are many common multiples of 3 and 4. We could have used 24 for example. But the **least** common multiple will provide the lowest common denominator that is easiest to use when adding and subtracting fractions. Using any other multiple usually means that there will be more simplification after you have performed the addition or subtraction.

Remember that the individual fractions will retain the same value only if the numerator and denominator are multiplied by the same value.

Multiplication of two fractions is a simpler operation because fractions multiply as follows:

$$^7/_8 \times {}^3/_4 = {}^{(7 \times 3)}/_{(8 \times 4)} = {}^{21}/_{32}$$

The fractional answer is in simplest form because there are no common factors. If common factors exist in the numerator and denominator of a fraction, then that fraction must be simplified.

Finally, division of fractions should never be attempted in the form of a ratio. The method is confusing and elaborate and unreliable in a testing situation. Instead, every fraction division can be a simple operation because the division operation can be rewritten as a multiplication as follows:

As noted previously, dividend / divisor = quotient.

This can be rewritten as:

dividend x ($^1/_{divisor}$) = quotient

which is the same outcome as division. The quantity ($^1/_{divisor}$) is called a reciprocal and for a fraction it is as simple as flipping the fraction upside down.

Therefore:

$$(^5/_8) / (^1/_4) = {}^5/_8 \times {}^4/_1 = {}^{20}/_8 = 2\,{}^4/_8 \text{ or } 2\,{}^1/_2 \text{ (in simplified form)}$$

When a series of arithmetic operations are listed one after another, there is an method used to standardize results. The abbreviation **PEMDAS** stands for:

Parentheses, Exponents, Multiplication, Division, Addition and Subtractions

Which is a list of arithmetic operations in order of priority. Clearly operations inside of parentheses are performed first, followed by exponents since they occur second on the list.

Multiplication and Division are performed with equal priority but in left to right order as they are read. Addition and Subtraction are also performed with equal priority but in left to right order as they are read in the same manner.

Hints:
- Look for parentheses and exponents first.
- Execute those items in the correct order.
- Rewrite expression with remaining multiplication, division, addition and subtractions.
- Execute the multiplication and division in left to right order.
- Rewrite expression with remaining addition and subtractions.
- Execute the addition and subtractions in left to right order.

If you have executed this series of instructions in PEMDAS order, you will have the correct answer. One excellent way to check is that **EVERY** PEMDAS problem, if executed correctly, always ends in a series of additions and subtractions. Assuming you rewrote the expression as recommended, you will be able to go back and check your work to reassure yourself and build your confidence.

M.1.3. Compare and order rational numbers

- Decimals and comparison, place value and significance
- Comparison with like denominators
- Comparison with unlike denominators

Comparing and ordering rational numbers is about the determination of the inequality of two ratios, or which is the greater or lesser of two ratios. There are multiple ways to determine the comparison between two ratios.

In section M.1.1, we discussed the process of converting ratios into decimals. If the ratios can be converted into decimal form, then the comparison is a simple. If you choose this process, the comparison is a simple matter of evaluating two decimals. It is important to relate the matter of significance when considering this method. The decimal 0.751 is greater than 0.75. This may seem obvious but the evaluation is only complete when noting that 0.75 is equal to 0.750 and 750 is less than 751. The comparison is evaluated by looking at the third decimal place behind the decimal point (thousandths place). That value of zero in that third decimal place does not exist in the original form of the decimal. But the zero is implied because of the blank in that decimal place. The additional zero is allowed when comparing decimal numbers.

If the rational numbers are left in ratio form, there are two distinct possible outcomes. First, if the ratios have the same denominator, then the comparison is simply a matter of comparing the numerators. The larger numerator is the larger ratio. Obviously, one – fourth is less than three - fourths. One – fourth is also less than two - fourths which is another name for one – half. In the case of differing denominators, if a common denominator can be readily determined, this form of comparison can still be used.

Finally, if there are two ratios that can't obviously be converted to a common denominator, there is another simple but effective measure to allow comparison. If the two ratios are $^a/_b$ and $^c/_d$, the simple process of cross multiplication will allow a comparison. If the product bd is used as the common denominator, then the first fraction becomes $^{ad}/_{bd}$ while the second fraction becomes $^{bc}/_{bd}$. The comparison then becomes whether product "ad" is greater than or less than the product "bc". These two products are achieved simply by cross multiplying the numerators and denominators and maintaining the order of the two products. The final comparison is based upon the common denominator idea, but the algorithm is a simple matter of executing the products and comparing the results. It is not a trick but a simple mathematical process.

M.1.4. Solve equations with one variable

- Variable on one side and numbers on the other side
- Same operations on both sides of the equal sign
- Algebraic equation
- Combine like terms
- Constant
- Inverse Arithmetic Operation
- Reciprocal
- Variable
- Variable Terms

Solving equations is a basic foundation of Algebra skills. The term "equation" means that in between two algebraic expressions there is an equal sign. Section M.1.10 contains a table of what expressions can be. Simply, on either side of the equal sign there will be combinations of numbers and variables in various forms. The equation is solved when a single variable is on one side of the equal sign and a numerical value is on the other side. The steps involve combining like terms and applying inverse arithmetic operations. When we say "combine like terms" we mean that numbers will be manipulated to be one side of the equal sign (by convention, usually the right side), while the variable remains on the other (usually left) side. This may seem like a very general requirement, but the overriding issue is to make sure that all manipulation is completed while the equality is maintained between the left and right side of the equation. The guideline is that equality will **always** be preserved as long as the same operation is performed on each side of the equal sign. The question of which operations must be performed is determined by the expressions that are present in the equation. Specifically, the inverse operations are chosen to provide the results which we have specified in this paragraph. A few simple examples will illustrate the necessary steps.

Example 1: In the equation

$$X + 9 = 64$$

...there is a variable expression on the left side and a constant on the right side. Our goal is to end with the variable alone on the left and a constant on the right. That means we need to eliminate the number nine that is added to the variable on the left side. Elimination of the number nine is achieved by using the inverse operation of the addition. Equality is preserved by subtracting the same number on both sides of the equal sign. Specifically:

$X + 9 - 9 = 64 - 9$

The result is that x = 55. Using that value in the original equation is a correct solution. Because the original equation had an addition, the solution required a subtraction.

Example 2: A slightly more complex equation involves multiple operations in the solution:

$$9a - 14 = 67$$

$$9a - 14 + 14 = 67 + 14$$

$$9a = 81$$

$$9a/9 = 81/9$$

The result is that a = 9. Using that value in the original equation is a correct solution. Because the original equation has a subtraction and a multiplication, the solution required addition and division to solve. Notice that the addition is performed first. The process can be solved in either order but doing the addition and subtraction first means that addition and subtraction of fractions will not be required later in the solution. Until now the examples had only one variable expression. You will see that more complex equations will be solved with the same methods.

Example 3: A slightly more complex equation involves variable expressions on both sides of the equation:

$$17t + 52 = 9t + 68$$

$$17t + 52 - 52 = 9t + 68 - 52$$

$$17t = 9t + 16$$

$$17t - 9t = 9t - 9t + 16$$

$$8t = 16$$

$$8t/8 = 16/8$$

$$t = 2$$

The result is that t = 2. Using that value in the original equation is a correct solution. Subtraction was used twice, once with the variable terms and once with the constant terms until a single variable expression was equal to a single constant. Only then was the division process used to find a single variable equal to a constant with the inverse operation to find the value of t.

Could this solution have been achieved if the division was performed first? Of course it could, but it would mean that the solution would involve fraction addition and subtraction for both the constant terms and the variable terms. The best guideline to help you remember the correct order is that addition and subtraction are performed until the constant term is on one side of the equal sign and the variable term is on the other side. Once they are on opposite sides, division by the coefficient in the variable term will determine the value of one variable.

M.1.5. Solve real world one or multiple step word problems with rational numbers

- Interpreting verbal descriptions
- Formulating relations (equations)
- Checking and solving

Ratios and fractions are synonymous when discussing numerical values. The ratios or fractions always imply division of the numerator by the denominator as stated previously. The numerical values of ratios routinely occur in the testing situation. In previous section M.1.1, the conversion between fractions and decimals and back to fractions was discussed. In this section, the discussion is directed towards how words appear in ratio problems and how those words should be interpreted.

A commonly used ratio, defined by specific words, is contained in the term "miles per hour", usually abbreviated by mph. When the term "miles per hour" is interpreted numerically it is the ratio of the total number of miles traveled divided by the number of hours traveled. More details of this ratio will be discussed when converting units. The key word in this commonly used term is "per". It literally means for each hour of travel a specific number of miles will be traveled. It has the same implication when the term is "gallons per hour" (how fast the tub is filled or the lawn is watered) or "tons per year" (how much ore is mined in one year).

Another way that ratios can appear is when a phrase defines a ratio of one value to another. A common comparison is usually the ratio of "men to women" or vice versa. Test problems will often use the ratio "boys to girls" or "girls to boys". When this terminology is used, the first term is in the numerator and the second term is in the denominator by convention.

There is an inherent problem when this terminology is used as illustrated by the example below:

In a classroom setting, the ratio of girls to boys is 3 to 4 (or 3:4 in strictly mathematical terms). How many boys are there in the classroom if the total number of students is 28?

There are two ways that this word problem may be easily solved. If the ratio of $^{girls}/_{boys}$ is ¾, the actual numbers may be ¾ or $^6/_8$ or $^9/_{12}$ or $^{12}/_{16}$ and so forth. These fractions are all equivalent fractions since they all simplify to the value of ¾. The equivalent fractions are easily determined as the ratios of multiples of the numerator and denominator of the original fraction. There is only one fraction where the numerator and denominator add to a total of 28 and that is the ratio $^{12}/_{16}$. Therefore, the solution is the classroom has 16 boys and 12 girls.

Notice that the words specify which group, boys or girls, is which specific number in the original problem and in the solution. When choosing multiple-choice answers, make sure that the correct number is chosen based upon the original definition in the problem. Most often both numerical values are in the answer choices and only one selection is correct.

M.1.6. Solve real world Problems involving percentages

- Percentages are special rational numbers
- Percentages are most easily used with decimal equivalents
- Percent Increase
- Percent decrease

Solving word problems with percentages begins with the concept that percentages are ratios. In section M.1.5 we solved problems with rational numbers so in this section the specifics of percentage problems will be addressed. Percentages are ratios with 100 in the denominator; the "per cent" or per 100. A group of 14 students in a grade level with 140 students is a ratio of 14/140 or 10%. In section M.1.1 we looked at formulating percentages from ratios and ratios from percentages. In this section we will apply percentages to solving real world problems where they are commonly used.

The most common percentage problems involve finding what percentage a number represents. In this section, reading precisely what is given and what is requested will be of extreme importance. For example, we may be asked to find the percentage of boys in a classroom if there are 18 boys and 22 girls. The key to formulating the correct ratio first is that the numerator is the total number of boys and the denominator is **the total number of students in the classroom!** Students are often misled to the formulation of a ratio using just the two numbers given. But the words of the question specify that the number of boys (18) be compared to the total number in the class. So the ratio becomes 18/40. That percentage is determined by performing the division and the result is a decimal value of 0.45 which is represented as 45%.

Now, what would it look like if the problem was presented in the opposite order. If it were given that there were 18 boys in the class and they represented 60 % of the class, how would that solution be formulated? The solution is simply a one-step solution like we have already solved. The constant part of the equation is the 18, while the variable part is 60% of the classroom size which we will call the variable "x". The solution becomes:

$$.60 \, x = 18$$

$$.60 \, x / .60 = 18 / .60$$

$$x = 30$$

If that question was reformulated with a slightly different wording, the mathematics would appear totally different. If instead you were given that only 20 students were in a class and you were asked to find the 60% of the class that were musicians the equations would appear as follows:

$$.60 * 20 = m$$

The solution is a simple multiplication with m = 12. But, you may not know that the simple solution works unless you formulate the equation guided by your understanding of the words that are in the problem. We have already seen how important the words are in ratio problems. Make sure that you read carefully and formulate an equation that is representative.

Another type of percentage question involves percent increase or decrease. You will see that this sort of problem involves quantifying a change relative to a given amount. Quite often this sort of problem involves money, so it's obvious that these problems will prove to be quite valuable.

For example, if the problem asks you to find your percent increase for your new raise that increases your pay from $10.00 to $13.50 per hour? In this case the unknown is the percent "p". The percent is defined as the ratio of the "increase"/ the original amount. Here again, there is a need to read carefully so that the comparison is understood completely. The equation looks like this:

$$P = (13.5 - 10) / 10$$

$$P = 3.5/10$$

$$P = 35\%$$

Did you remember to move the decimal point to make the decimal the percent? Notice that the subtraction was necessary to provide the "amount of change". Dividing that amount by the original pay rate provides the percent change.

We have addressed the "percent increase" question and the remaining question is about the opposite type of problem where we are asked to quantify the "percent decrease". As you might have guessed, the numerator will be another subtraction so we can calculate the decreased amount. As before, we are using the original amount as the denominator but in this case, it is the larger of the two values. So finding the percent decrease problems are solved as follows:

If your savings has has balance of $275 some of that total is deducted to pay bank service fees. If the new account balance is $263, what was the percent decrease in the account? The equation becomes:

$$P = (275 - 263)/275$$

$$P = 12/275$$

$$P = 4.4\% \text{ approximately}$$

Notice the beginning amount is in the denominator and the changed amount is in the numerator. Reading carefully is important once again to ensure that our ratio contains the correct amounts for the percentage calculation

M.1.7. Apply estimation strategies and rounding rules to real-world problems

- Rounding and significance
- Estimation and precision
- Primarily Metric system
- Distance
- Mass
- Temperature

In the world of quantifying numerical values, it is very common for us to estimate and round numbers for everyday use. If we are asked our age, we typically would not respond with the number of years, months, weeks and days. Of course we normally express our age in whole number of years. But also in that process we may round our age to the nearest year and that leads to the first topic in this section. When we are rounding a numerical value, we would normally want to understand the precision that is required. An example of the rounding process follows:

Example 1: Our calculated value when we solve a problem comes out to 256.739.

If we are asked to round to the nearest whole number, the 7 in the tenths place tells us that the whole number would be expressed as 257. A number in the tenths place equal to 5 or greater means that the ones place would be rounded to the next higher value. If it had been 4 or or less in the tenths place it would have remained at 256.

If our value is significantly more precise than needed, we may be asked to round to the nearest hundred. In that case, the 5 in the tens place means that the rounded value would be 300. Again the rounding rule is the same as the previous example except that it is applied to the number in the tens place.

In the world of scientific measurement, the precision is typically determined by the device used for the measurement. A metric balance scale would be more precise than required to weigh the amount of meat for a burger. Conversely, using a bathroom scale to measure a medical dose would never be considered precise enough. Having an introduction to precision helps us to estimate quantities. The difficult part is that for most of the scientific world, those estimations need to be within the metric system. We will use some examples to provide a means for you to compare your estimations. We will organize this discussion around the metric system units that you may be expected to use.

The largest unit of measure that you may be asked to use, is the kilometer. It is about 5/8ths of a mile so if you are asked to estimate your bus ride to school, you could take the number of miles and multiply by 8 and divide by 5. The decimal conversion is that a kilometer is about .625 miles or a mile is about 1.6 kilometers. A way to remember the conversion is that 55 miles per hour is approximately 88 kilometers per hour.
Shorter distances may be easier to convert and estimate. A meter is close to 39 inches or about 10% more than a yard. A football field then is about 110 meters.

The centimeter is one of the most useful units of metric measure. A way to compare is that 10 centimeters is close to 4 inches. 1 centimeter is very close to 3/8ths of an inch. An inch is about 25.4 millimeters. Since inches are usually broken down into sixteenths and thirty- seconds, a millimeter is easy to picture as a length between those small units that we often find on a tape measure or a ruler.

This discussion has provided some images that should help you in your effort to become fluent in using the metric system of length measurement. Unlike the standard system of measurement that is used in the U.S., there is a logical progression with powers of ten describing the relationship between these metric units we have discussed. Even better, the units of mass have a similar and logical relationship. Larger masses would typically be weighed in kilograms and small quantities would be weighed in grams. From your prior knowledge, you may remember that the relationship between a kilometer and a meter is 1000 m/km. In mass measurement the relationship is similar, 1000g/kg is the conversion. Relative to each other, we can compare and relate but the connections to real world objects may not be so obvious. However, it is actually simpler in the metric system than the standard system.

When the metric system was formulated, the unit of the gram was defined as the mass of one cubic centimeter of water. A cubic centimeter is about a teaspoon of water, so a gram is a very small unit of mass. A medical dose in a pill may be less than, but comparable to, a gram. But it provides a relative size to help you estimate. A letter in the mail may weigh a few grams. A milk carton is about a couple of kilograms. A soda bottle is just under a liter or 1000 cubic centimeters, so it weighs about 800 grams. Remember, your estimation may not be exactly the same as someone else's. But the comparisons from your knowledge base will increase the quality of your estimation.

Converting temperatures between Fahrenheit and Celsius scales can be accomplished using formulas that would be cumbersome for estimation purposes. They are however, linear scales that have a few points that will allow you to estimate temperatures that are close to the given values. Look at the following table for comparison:

F°	C°	
32	0	Freezing water
68	20	Cool Room
86	30	Warm day
212	100	Boiling water

Remember, you are estimating temperatures. Do you have an estimate for 50° C (halfway between 32 and 212)? Would you be comfortable at a temperature of 10° C? (halfway between 32 and 68)? To find the number halfway between add the two numbers and divide by two. 50° C is about 122° F and 10° C is about 50° F. Estimating is a challenge for everyone but practice makes everyone better and we all develop confidence when we practice.

M.1.8. Solve real world Problems involving proportions

- Proportion and ratios
- Constant of Proportionality

In previous sections, the topic of ratios has been addressed in various ways. In this section, real world examples will help you apply this to your problem solving. There are two features of all proportionality problems that you will use. First, proportionality means that two quantities will always compare in a constant ratio. This ratio is called the constant of proportionality (k) and it is often depicted as follows:

$$Y = K*X$$

And therefore:

$$K = Y/X$$

This may seem to be just a simple observation but in fact it results in a powerful problem solving tool. The following examples will illustrate how the proportionality is used.

A common example is the pay that is received for the hours that are worked. That ratio of dollars per hour is what we normally consider our rate of pay. If your rate is $17.50 per hour, then the following rates will apply:

$35/2   ($35 for 2 hours worked)
$87.50/5   ($87.50 for 5 hours worked)
$437.50/25   ($437.50 for 25 hours worked

How much money would you be paid for a 40-hour work week? The ratios that could be used are almost unlimited in number, but **one** solution would be as follows:

$$\$17.50/1 = X / 40$$

$$40 * \$17.50 = \$700.00$$

Of course this is a simple problem, but to illustrate how ratios are used, the problem could be solved with any of the other of the ratios:

$$\$437.50/25 = X / 40$$

$$25 X = \$437.50 * 40 \qquad \text{(cross multiplying)}$$

$$X = \$437.50 * 40/25$$

$$X = \$700$$

This is a simple example, but it illustrates an extremely valuable property of proportionality in problem solving. Once the proportionality constant is established, the rest of the problem solving is cross multiplying and dividing. The same answer resulted from using different numbers but they originated with the same proportionality constant.

Another example is to use proportionality to determine the completion of a work scope. If your workforce is able to generate 550 widgets (a common but fictional product) in a single 8-hour work day, how many hours are required to complete an order of 1750 widgets for your best customer?

The ratios are as follows:

$$550 / 8 = 1750 / X$$

$$550 * X = 1750 * 8 \quad \text{(cross multiplying)}$$

$$X = 1750 * 8 / 550$$

$$X = 25.45 \text{ hours}$$

This number tells you the how many hours are required to complete the order. There may be other questions to consider. The distribution of approximately 25-1/2 hours (rounded because we would never worry about .05 hours) is another question. The basic proportionality problem provides the information needed for the other real world questions of overtime or extra workers to be addressed separately.

M.1.9. Solve real world Problems involving ratios and rates of change

- Rate
- Rate of change
- Ratio
- Unit Rate

Ratios have appeared in previous sections and we know that fractions, ratios and even rational numbers are all linked by the concept of a number divided by another number. We have used these ratios in mathematical problem solving examples. In this section our ratios will serve another purpose. Understanding the concept of rate give us another powerful problem solving tool. Understanding the terminology associated with rates and ratios is the first step in problem applications.

The term "rate", is defined as the ratio of two quantities with different units of measure. We used a pay rate in section M.1.8 because it is familiar to everyone. It represents "R" the number of dollars per hour that are earned for working. We also know if that we work "X" number hours we will earn R*X dollars for our efforts. If we double the number of hours, we earn double the amount of money. In terms of the rate "R", for each hour that is worked the rate of change in dollars earned is "R" the number of dollars per hour. Since "R" is the amount of money "per hour", it represents something called a "Unit Rate". As we shall see, this term is commonly applied even when we do not use the term.

Another widely used rate system is the one associated with driving a car. If we are driving and the speedometer reads 65, it means that we are moving at a rate of 65 miles per hour (mph). In terms of "rate" terminology, the rate of change in the position of our car, is 65 mph. In one hour our car will be 65 miles from the current location. Notice that 65 mph is a unit rate because the motion is 65 miles **per single hour.** Finally, for every hour that we apply the 65 mph rate, the car will be 65 miles further down the road. Simple examples will demonstrate the problem solving methods.

For example, at the 65mph rate, how much time (T) is required to travel 250 miles one way? The equation is modeled after "distance equals rate multiplied by time". The solution becomes:

$$250 = 65 * T$$

$$250/65 = T * 65/65$$

$$T = 3.85 \text{ hours (rounded)}$$

Note that this is not 3 hours and 85 minutes. Since 60 minutes are in one hour, .85 * 60 = 51 minutes (approximately). Our trip will take 3 hours and 51 minutes.

A similar example is how fast must we drive if we need to travel the 250 miles in 2 hours and 45 minutes? The equation becomes:

$$250 = R * 2.75 \text{ (45 minutes is ¾ or .75 hours)}$$

$$250 / 2.75 = R * 2.75 / 2.75$$

$$250 = R * 2.75$$

$$R = 91 \text{ mph} \qquad \text{(90.9 rounded to mph)}$$

If that sounds fast, it's a great lesson. Even though the correct ratios can be formulated, it doesn't mean that the ratio will be "reasonable".   We can achieve 91 mph but traveling at that speed is not a reasonable outcome normally.

The rate problem leads to another example that is asked in a workplace situation. If you are in charge of workers, you may be asked to use this type of calculation to determine how to get the required productivity. The problem is to determine the rate of completion of a given task. Workers may have different rates of productivity in the workplace. We may be asked to combine the efforts of workers to finish in a shorter time.

In this example, worker A can complete a task working alone in 8 hours and worker B can complete the same task in 5 hours. How long will it take for them to complete the task if they work together? The individual rate for worker A is 1 task per 8 hours or 1/8 task/hour. Worker B completes 1 task per 5 hours or 1/5 task/hour. Their combined rate is 1/5 + 1/8 or 13/40 task /hour (remember the section where we found common denominators?) The final solution in the form of rate * time is as follows:

$$1 \text{ completed task} = 13/40 \text{ task/hour} *T \text{ (the task completion time)}$$

$$T = 40 / 13 \text{ (3.077 rounded)}$$

This solution says that the combined effort will require about 3 hours and 6 minutes (rounding to the nearest tenth of an hour). This may not seem to be intuitive or "reasonable". However, it's simply the outcome when the workers have two different work rates. Using two workers with the same rate would mean that the required time would be half the completion time for one worker. That makes sense intuitively but the mathematics allows you to evaluate the more complex problems.

M.1.10. Translate phrases and sentences into expressions, equations, and inequalities

- Equation (means a single answer)
- Expression
- Inequality (means ranges of answers that satisfy the condition "greater than or less than")
- Simplify

Algebra uses variables, numbers and operations as the basic parts. Variables are typically represented by letters and may have any number of values in a problem. Usually the variable is the unknown quantity in a problem. All letters can and often are used, but x, y, and z are letters that appear most often in algebra textbooks. In a testing situation, letters other than x, y, and z are often used to mislead test takers.

Algebraic expressions are variables and numbers with operations such as addition, subtraction, multiplication and division. The following are all examples of algebraic expressions:

x	y	a	(letters)
$7u$	$\frac{1}{2}q$	$3.9\,p$	(product of a variable and number)
$s + 5$	$u+v$	$2.3+r$	(sum of a variable and number)
$z - 3.5$	$k-n$	$t - 1.3$	(difference of a variable and number)
$m/6$	$z/2$	$3.9/p$	(quotient of a variable and number)
c^2	$b^{0.5}$	$\sqrt{3}$	(variable or number w/ an exponent)

Notably, the sum, difference, product or quotient of these items are also expressions.

Equations are defined as algebraic expressions that are set equal to a number, variable or another expression. The simplest identifier of an equation is the equal sign (=). When an equation is written to express a condition or represent a situation for problem solving, the solution is normally completed by manipulating the equation correctly so that a variable or unknown quantity is on one side of the equal sign and the numerical answer (s) are on the other side of the equal sign.

An example of an expression is "X – 35". An equation results if that expression is set equal to a number or another expression. For example, a simple equation results if "X – 35" is set equal to the number 78. To solve that equation, we use the steps from M.1.5. Our answer becomes X = 113. That value establishes the value of X that makes the left side equal to the right side. The reason that this terminology is important is that we need to determine what happens when we establish an Inequality.

If the equation was changed to an inequality, the result would be either the expression "greater than" or "less than" the numerical value on the other side of the sign. In the case of the inequality, there are signs which we use for "less than" or "greater than" as follows:

"<" means the left side is less than the right side

">"   means the left side is greater than the right side

These signs are normally read left to right. It can be confusing but, there is a definitive way to make sure that the signs are interpreted correctly. Simply, the signs when viewed as arrowheads, always point toward the smaller side. Evaluating these "inequalities" is simply a matter of solving the equality and checking to see if the result is consistent with the original inequality. In the example of

$$X - 35 > 95$$

$$X - 35 + 35 > 95 + 35$$

$$X > 130$$

This solution means that any value greater than 130 means that the original inequality is true. Solving other inequalities is similar. If it is necessary to multiply both sides of and equation by a negative number to solve, then the direction of the inequality sign is reversed. If you check your result for reasonableness, the correct value will provide the correct result.

Expressions may require simplification. In this section we look at the methods of simplification that may be useful as steps to problem solution.

In the expression:

$$8X + 18$$

there are common factors that allow the expression to be simplified. Since 8 and 18 are both even numbers they have a common factor of 2. Therefore, the expression is simplified by writing it as follows:

$$2(4x+9)$$

The common factor appears outside the parentheses and the 4 and the 9 are left inside since they have no common factors.

If that expression was:

$$8X + 16$$

the common factor could be 2 ,or 4, or 8. Choosing the largest common factor provides the best choice for simplification.

Another simplification example is a rational expression with common factors in the numerator and denominator. The rational expression:

$$X^7 / X^3$$

can be simplified into just: $\qquad\qquad X^4$

To illustrate how this simplification occurs, we can rewrite the original expression in expanded form:

$$X^7 / X^3 = X^4 * X/X*X/X*X/X$$

In the expanded form, there are seven "X" factors in the numerator and three "X" factors in the denominator. Clearly the three factors of X/X can be cancelled since they always equal one. The remaining factor is the simplified form of the expression.

After looking at the simplification of expressions, a few examples will be used to illustrate problem-solving methods.

If the simple equation is written in word form, the first step must be to write the equation that represents that written question. The simple problem of ages of individuals is a common example:

Example 1: Jane is 8 years older than Nancy. In 5 years she will be 27 years old. What is Jane's age now?

The variable J will represent Jane's age and the expression J+5 will represent Jane's age in 5 years. In this example we read that this expression is equal to a number, in this case 27. Our equation becomes:

$$J+5 = 27$$

In the words of the problem, we have the correct expression set equal to a number. Our basic principle is to perform algebraic operations until the "J" is alone on one side of the equation and the numerical answer is on the other side. This type of solution involves the opposite of the addition (+5) so 5 is subtracted from both sides.

$$
\begin{array}{r}
J+5 = 27 \\
\underline{-5 \quad -5} \\
J+0 = 22
\end{array}
$$

Therefore, the answer says that Jane's age is now 22 years of age. What happened to Nancy's age? Often, extraneous information is left in the problem as a distractor from the problem at hand. In Example 2, the more complex version of this problem will be addressed.

If the simple equation involved a multiplication the steps would involve an opposite operation which in this case would be division such as:

$$
\begin{array}{c}
7J= 84 \\
7J /7 = 84/7 \\
J = 12
\end{array}
$$

These examples are typical of "one step solutions" since a single operation is involved to solve the problem.

Of course, there are multiple step solutions in more involved problems. But the rules are still the same, i.e.

- Opposite (or inverse) operations are performed to solve
- The same operations must be performed on both sides of the equation.
- The solution is complete when a variable is on one side and the numbers are on the other side

Example 2: Jane is 8 years older than Nancy. In 5 years she will be twice as old as Nancy. What is Jane's age now?

The first step to solving this type of problem is to identify the variable. In this solution we will select the variable "J" to represent Jane's age and "N" to represent Nancy's age.

The two equations from the word description, become:
$$J - 8 = N$$
$$\text{and}$$
$$J + 5 = 2(N+5)$$

Dividing both sides of the second equation by 2 means that it becomes:
$$(J+5)/2 = N+5$$
Adding 5 to the original equation we have:
$$J - 8 + 5 = N + 5$$

In this method, there are two expressions which contain "J" and they are both equal to "N + 5". Mathematically, they must be equal to each other. The completed equality becomes:
$$J - 3 = (J + 5)/2$$

To solve, multiply both sides by 2 (same operation on both sides) and the equation is:
$$2J - 6 = J + 5$$

Subtract J and add 6 to both sides and the answer becomes:

$$
\begin{array}{rcl}
2J - 6 & = & J + 5 \\
-J + 6 & & -J + 6 \\
\hline
J & = & 11
\end{array}
$$

With this solution, the problem is completed and the following statements are clarified:
- Now Jane is 11 years old and Nancy is 3 years old.
- In 5 years Jane will be 16 years old and Nancy will be 8 years old.

We are able to answer the question, "What is Jane's age now?" and all the other ages in the question because of an algebra principle that requires two equations for two unknowns. In the problem, there are two variables (J and N) and two relationships between them (now and 5 years from now). If we are able to formulate two equations with the two unknowns, then algebra principles will allow for the solution of a complex problem.

M.2.1. MEASUREMENT AND DATA

Interpret relevant information from tables, charts, and graphs:

- Axis
- Bivariate
- Cartesian Coordinate
- Chart
- Graph
- Legend
- Scale
- Table

In this section, the important systems for presenting data in graphic ways will be discussed. The purpose of the tables, charts or graphs is to formulate a representation of specific data in a system that is informative and meaningful to an audience or in the workplace to coworkers who may not have had direct contact with the presented data. An often overlooked benefit of presenting data in these forms is to allow trending, interpolation and extrapolation based upon the existing data. If these terms are not familiar to you now, they will be discussed after some basic concepts are presented.

Graphic data is normally presented on an x-y coordinate system. The x values are normally scaled on the horizontal number line called the "x axis". The vertical axis is the "y axis". The scale of the two axes does not necessarily need to be exactly the same. Plotting real data often means that the axes will be different because the x and y data will use numerically different data. If there are differing he scales of the axes, this information would normally be included in the label for the individual axis. The labels may include the units (cm for example), a scale factor (100's of mm), and the type of data represented. The data presented is termed "bivariate" because there are two variables that are paired together in the presentation of the data. Before the data is plotted on this two axis system, it is normally represented in "x-y pairs" which are written as ordered pairs inside of parentheses (x, y). Often, students are confused on the formulation of the ordered pairs. The guidelines will be discussed for you to apply when your data is ready to plot.

The ordered pairs are usually gathered in (x, y) form, where the x value is first and the y value is second inside the parentheses. The horizontal axis is always first and the vertical axis is always second. If there is some confusion, the "x, y" pair is always in alphabetical order, x first, y second. These two values are normally referred to as Cartesian coordinates and the graphing system is called the Cartesian plane. The horizontal axis is normally used to plot the "independent" data, and the vertical axis is use to plot the "dependent" data. A medical example is an excellent way to illustrate how data is categorized as dependent or independent.

A critical patient may have his vital signs taken several times a day. When plotted, the data would be presented with the time of day on the x axis and the blood pressure, for example, on the vertical axis. For clarity, the horizontal axis would be labeled, "time", along with the AM / PM format (24-hour time formats are standard in the military). The vertical axis would be labeled "blood pressure" and probably include both systolic and diastolic values as two different points for single timed entry.

If this is not enough to clarify the choice for "x data" and "y data", then it may be worthwhile to use this questioning method to help you decide. In the case of the vital signs, do the vital signs depend on the time of day or does the time of day depend on the vital signs? The second part of this question is silly, so the vital signs are dependent and are graphed on the y axis. The time is graphed on the x axis. If there is any question on the formulation of the graph, a legend is normally used so the viewer has a clear picture of the intent and content of the graph. In the example of the critical care patient, it would possibly be labeled "Blood Pressure Data for Marcus Jones, May 19 – 21, 2016". The patient's name means that the graph is dedicated to his folder and the dates allow the graph to be viewed relative to previous and subsequent blood pressure data. More specific information will be discussed in the section below discussing evaluation of data.

If the plotted data is depicted in the form of a connected line between data points, it would normally be called a line graph or just a graph. There are two other forms of data representation. They can be shown on a coordinate axis such as the original data graph. If the data is demonstrated in the form of solid vertical bars the data is in chart form for a display called a histogram. If multiple data items are depicted with adjacent vertical bars, the display form is called a bar chart. Both of these displays are typically done on graph paper but instead of the line, the representation is simplified in the form of vertical bars. A significant benefit in this data form is the possible use of color the further enhance the significance of your data display.

Another type of chart is valuable for multiple data items that can be viewed as "parts of a whole". If we are depicting budgetary items, for example, a pie chart is often used for viewing the items that make up the total budget. The term "piece of the pie", refers to the concept of parts of the whole in the shape of pie slices. Again, a legend is used to clarify the percentages of the "pie slices" and the description of the budgetary items represented. In the makeup of the pie chart the central angle of each item is directly proportional to the percentage represented. A 35% item in a budget would have a central angle determined by 35% of the 360° in the full circle. In this case the central angle would be .35*360° or 126°. The complete pie represents 100% of the budget and the sum of all the budgetary items.

A final representation can be very useful in the form of a table. The following example will be analyzed to show how useful a table can be:

X	Y
5	7
11	19
14	25
23	43

Of course, this table could be used as the basis for a graph on a Cartesian coordinate system. In the following sections, examples such as this will be used to demonstrate how valuable trending data can be determined by direct analysis of the table itself.

M.2.2. Evaluate the information in tables, charts, and graphs using statistics.

- Measures of central tendency
- Outlier
- Range
- Shape
- Spread
- Data Trend
- Expected value (Interpolate and Extrapolate)
- Point on a graph

In a set of numerical data, the concept of central tendency is an important quality with several different ways that it may be characterized. Mean, median, mode and range are commonly used terms of central tendency that are defined and demonstrated in this section.

To determine the Mean, the elements of the data set are simply added together and that sum is divided by the total number of items in the set. You may have used the word "average" to describe this same quality and the two are the same calculation. It is possibly the most known quantity and has simple yet powerful applications.

In the first example, the number set will be defined as follows:

$$6, 5, 8, 11, 23, 14, 7, 9$$

In this calculation, the order of the sample need not be considered. The next step is to find the sum of the sample:

Sum of the sample = 83

$$83/ 8 = 10.375 \text{ (rounded to 10.4)}$$

Dividing by 8, the sample mean is 10.4. It is important to note from this example that the mean is not necessarily an element of the original set. We can use the calculated mean value to compare with the other central tendencies to be determined.

To determine the median, the numbers of the set must first be assembled in order. The given set, in order, appears as follows;

$$5, 6, 7, 8, 9, 11, 14, 23$$

Once the set is ordered, the median is the number that appears exactly in the middle of the set with equal numbers of the set to the left and the right of median. Note that the given set in this problem has an even number of elements. In this case the median is determined to be the average of the two center elements. In this sample the two center elements are 8 and 9 so the average of the two and therefore the median is 8.5.

The mode of a set is the number that appears most often in the set. Specifically, the mode must appear at least twice and in this set the mode is undefined.

The range of the set is sometimes considered as measure of central tendency. It is defined as the largest element of set minus the smallest element. In our example above, the range is defined as:

$$23 - 5 = 18$$

The range in this example is once again not an element of the set. Further in most cases it is the least likely to represent the original set of data. If the data is represented on a number line or as a bar graph of data, the range is a measure of the spread from the greatest to the least of the data elements.

In this section the data sets have been limited in number, depicting only eight elements in the sample. For samples that are larger in number, there are qualities of the set that can be viewed as shapes of the data distribution. The normal distribution is a large set of numbers with as single peak in the distribution and symmetrical values mirroring the data on the opposite side of the peak. Sometimes called the "bell curve", the ideal distribution has the mean, median and mode centered at the central value of the distribution. With a table of the "Standard Normal Distribution" models of the "bell curve" type of distribution can be quantified numerically. For the purposes of this discussion the shape of the curve will be adequate to describe the distribution. If there are two peaks in this distribution, it is called "bi-modal". In the previous discussion of the mode, the values were the ones that appeared most often. The mode is the value that has the highest peak of the distribution and if there are two or more peaks, the data is said to be "bimodal" (or multi-modal for more peaks).

In the analysis of the shape of the data sets, there may be an asymmetry to the shape which is a quality called skewness. If there is an excess of data to the left of the distribution (with data tailing to the left of the main peak of the distribution) it is said to be "skewed left". The opposite condition is called "skewed right". Skewness is a common feature of a data distribution in the real world. If the skewed data can be characterized as a single data point, (an extreme case) that data point is called an outlier. Once a data point is labeled as an outlier, it is not unusual that the qualities of the data distribution would be quantified without using the single outlier data point.

There are two other types of data sets to be considered when discussing the shape. If the data has no clear peaks and no identifiable trends it is termed a "uniform" distribution. Throughout the range of the data, there is a uniform number of data points at each value. The data is said to be "without trend" or "correlation".

If the data has a randomness but has a tendency to decrease to the right, the trend is said to be negative (as in the slope of the graph) or a negative correlation. If there is a tendency for the data to increase to the right, the trend is positive or increasing with a positive correlation. This level of evaluation is extremely valuable for characterizing experimental data that is expected to be "linear" in nature.

Further, a single straight line drawn along and following the trend of the random data is called a "line of bet fit". This is a graphic method for the purposes of this instruction, but advanced mathematical analysis or calculators can perform this estimation precisely for a limited data set. This technique is a valuable tool, since the line of best fit will allow the user to predict a y value for any value on the x axis. A point on the line of best fit allows for interpolation, the determination of a point between two actual data points. By extending the line of best fit past the range of the original date set, a point on the line can be used to extrapolate or predict values beyond the range of the original data.

The specifics of this simplified method of characterizing experimental data, is often the basis for analyzing simple high school level physics problems. The effectiveness of this method makes it valuable in the analysis of real world data.

A data table may not seem to be a representation useful for data analysis. The previous example will be used to demonstrate how a table can be used to illustrate linear data qualities.

This table was used earlier in this section:

X	Y
5	7
11	19
14	25
23	43

Of course, this table could be used as the basis for a graph on a Cartesian coordinate system but to find rate of change we can look at how variables change with the following work on the table:

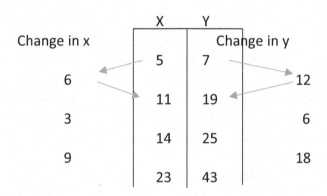

The rate of change in the table is defined as Change in y/ Change in x. On a graph this quantity is called the slope and provides a measure of how fast the data is rising or falling (if negative). The entries in the "Change in x" (and Change in y) columns are just the difference between the two adjacent x or y entries in the table. Any table that you encounter can be analyzed in this manner. The linearity is not obvious in the original table but the simple analysis in this example shows that the data is linear in nature, with a slope of positive 2 and a positive correlation.

In earlier examples we discussed interpolation and extrapolation in the data and the example can be used to demonstrate these qualities for a data table.

	X	Y	
Change in x	5	7	Change in y
	11	19	
	14	25	
	23	43	

Knowing that the slope is 2 allows you to determine a y value for x = 17. For x = 17 the change in x is 3 (measured from 14). Knowing that the Change in y/ Change in x is 2 means that the change in y must be 6 (measured from 25).   Therefore, the value for x = 17 would be y = 31 simply using the numerical values from the table. Since x=17 is inside the range of the data, this is interpolation.

Extrapolation, finding data points that are outside the range of the table, is also possible with this method. Can you see that x = 37 and y = 71 is an extension of the linear table that we began with in this section?

M.2.3. Explain the relationship between two variables.

- Covariance (positive and negative)
- Dependent variable
- Independent variable

The nature of the dependent and independent variable was discussed in section M.2.1. The topic of covariance will be explained with selected example to illustrate the concepts associated with covariance.

Covariance is defined as the property of how two variables change relative to each other. Since we have stated that y values are dependent and x values are independent, this becomes more of a description of how y changes with x.

Covariance of a data set that has a tendency to decrease to the right, is said to have a negative trend (as in the slope of the graph) or a negative covariance. If there is a tendency for the data to increase to the right, the trend is positive and increasing with a positive covariance. This level of evaluation is extremely valuable for characterizing experimental data that is expected to be "linear" in nature.   The concept of covariance and correlation for the purposes of this text are the same. Only with more advanced data analysis would these two concepts differ. For this reason, most secondary education focuses on correlation rather than covariance.

M.2.4. Calculate geometric qualities

- Linear Units
- Length
- Arc
- Subtend
- Circumference
- Perimeter
- Area
- Irregular Shape
- Square Units
- Sum
- Surface Area

In this section on geometric qualities, the general focus will be on one-dimensional and two-dimensional geometry. The specific focus will be on length and area. Under the heading of length and area, we can formulate a substantial knowledge base to problem solve real world geometric questions. This study will not address three dimensional objects and their volume or surface area.

Section M.1.7. contained the information on length units of measure in both the standard and metric systems. The length units of measurement are an important beginning of the geometry discussion because the two geometry topics apply the linear units of measure directly. Perimeter is defined as the distance around the outside of a two dimensional figure. A two dimensional figure is one that can be completely contained in a single plane. For this reason, they are sometime called planar figures

For example, the perimeter of a square is the sum of the four sides. Since the sides are equal in length, the perimeter of the square is the length of one side multiplied by four. In general, the perimeter is the sum of the length of all sides of the planar figure. This assumes that the sides are all line segments.

To determine the distance around the outside of a circle requires a quantity known as π (the Greek letter pi). The quantity π is defined as the ratio of the circumference / diameter for every circle. Therefore, the circumference which is the length of the outside curve of a circle is found by multiplying π times the diameter. The diameter is simply the straight line distance from one side to the other side of a circle, measured through the center. The curved segment which is part of a circumference is known as an arc. The arc length is a fraction of the circumference. That length is calculated with the following formula:

$$\text{Arc length} = \pi * \text{diameter} * \text{central angle} / 360°$$

The central angle is the angle with the center at the vertex. The central angle rays cut (or subtend) that part of the circumference that is in the interior of the angle. The ratio of that central angle / 360 is the fraction of the circumference. Can you see that the arc length of a semi-circle (1/2 of the circle) is π * diameter/2 or just π * radius? This π ratios is usually approximated as 3.14 although it is actually an irrational number with an unlimited number of decimal places. In this case it is precisely known as a ratio but never precisely known as a single number. In the following discussion of area, the ratio π appears in the formula for the area of a circle.

The concept of surface area begins with the length unit of the side of the figure. The shape that is considered the basis of area calculation is the square that measures one unit in length for each side. That unit may be metric or standard, but the square unit is defined as the measure of space inside that unit square. As we measure larger and more complex shapes, including circles, the areas will all be expressed in terms of square units.

The following table is a summary of the formulas for the area calculations associated with the triangular and quadrilateral shapes:

Square	$A = L * L = L^2$	L is the length of the side
Rectangle	$A = L * w$	L and w are the different side lengths
Isosceles Triangle	$A = \frac{1}{2} b * h$	b is the base length, h is the Perpendicular distance to the opposite Vertex.
Parallelogram	$A = b * h$	b is the base length, h is the Perpendicular distance to the opposite Side
Trapezoid	$A = \frac{1}{2} (b_1 + b_2) * h$	b_1 and b_2 are the two base length, h is the Perpendicular distance between the bases
Rhombus	$A = \frac{1}{2} (d_1 + d_2)$	d_1 and d_2 are the lengths of the diagonals

To determine the area inside of a circle again requires the quantity π. Instead of the diameter, the area calculation for a circle uses the radius which one half the diameter. It is defined as the distance from the center of the circle to the circumference. The area is calculated with the formula of π times the radius squared or $\pi * r^2$. The units are the square unit of the radius, either standard or metric.

The shapes that have been discussed in this section may be used to add and subtract from each other to calculate the area of complex shapes. The following examples will illustrate these methods.

Example 1: Find the area inside a rectangle but outside the circle in the diagram (not to scale):

The rectangle has length of 6cm and width of 5cm

The circle has radius of 2cm

Area of the rectangle is 5*6 = 30 cm^2

Area of the circle is π * 2*2 = 4 π cm^2

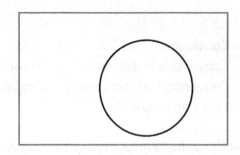

The required area is 30 - 4 π cm^2

If you expected a single number, the value of 3.14 can be used for π and the decimal value becomes:

$$30 - 12.56 = 17.44 \text{ cm}^2$$

Remember that the decimal number is not a precise answer. The answer that has the "pi" in the answer is a precise answer.

Example 2: Find the area inside the circle but outside the square in the diagram (not to scale):

The radius of the circle is 3"

The length of the side is 3"

Area of the square is 3*3 = 9 sq. inches

Area of the circle is π * 3*3= 9 π sq. inches

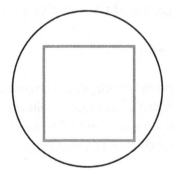

The required area is 9 π − 9 sq. inches

Again If you expected a single number, the value of 3.14 can be used for π and the decimal value becomes:

$$28.26 - 9 = 19.26 \text{ cm}^2$$

The combinations of all figures is impossible to duplicate in a limited text, but the concept of adding and subtracting areas and perimeters is a simple matter of identifying the specific parts that need to be added or subtracted. As you can see simple creativity is needed!

- Conversion
- Conversion factors within the standard or metric system.
- Conversion factors between standard and metric systems.
- Unit Conversion

Converting the units of measured or calculated quantities is simply a multiplication process that allows data to be presented in the preferred units of measure. The multiplication is simple if the conversion factor is known. A simple example of this process using familiar, well known units of measure will be helpful.

A football field is 100 yards from goal line to goal line. If we are asked to convert this measurement to feet, we know that there are 3 feet in every yard. The mathematical conversion factor is 3 $^{feet}/_{yard}$. The method to convert looks like this:

$$100 \, ^{yards}/_{field} * 3 \, ^{feet}/_{yard} = 300 \, ^{yards}/_{yard} * ^{feet}/_{field} = 300 \, ^{feet}/_{field}$$

In the conversion, the "yards" units cancel each other since one is in the numerator and one is in the denominator. The final units are left in the form that is required to answer the question in feet. This cancellation process not only tells us how to calculate but it also helps us to decide whether to multiply or divide. Writing the conversion factor with the units in the form of a ratio will help us decide on the process to use. Since 3 $^{feet}/_{yard}$ has feet in the numerator, it also shows us that the yards will cancel and the conversion process will provide the information that we require.

Can you see that this football field is also 3600 inches long?

To illustrate the other way that conversion factors may be used, we need to solve the problem of expressing this same football field in terms of miles. The readily known conversion factor is 5280 $^{feet}/_{mile}$. Since we need "miles" to be in the numerator, the conversion factor tells us that we must divide by 5280 $^{feet}/_{mile}$. The method to convert looks like this:

$$300 \, ^{feet}/_{field} * 1/5280 \, ^{mile}/_{feet} = 300/5280 \, ^{miles}/_{field} = 0.062 \text{ miles (rounded)}$$

That's not even a tenth of a mile!

Within the standard system of measurement, most of the conversion factors are quantities that we know. Feet, inches, yards and miles are well known by most people that need to measure or calculate data. The other type of conversion involves the metric system and converting standard units to metric. The main unit of conversion is 2.54 $^{centimeters}/_{inch}$. The football field that is 3600 inches long can be converted to centimeters as follows:

$$3600 \, ^{inches}/_{field} * 2.54 \, ^{centimeters}/_{inch} = 9144 \text{ centimeters}$$

The conversion to other units within the metric system is simplified by the fact that the units contain the information that helps choose the conversion factor. For example, the centimeter units that we used contain the metric prefix "centi" which means one hundredth. Therefore, the 9144 centimeters in the football field is converted as follows:

$$9144 \text{ centimeters } *1/100 \ ^{meter}/_{centimeters} = 91.44 \text{ meters}$$

That also tells you that a meter is about 91 % of a yard.

If we need to look at the field in terms of a kilometer, the prefix "kilo" means one thousand so, the 91.44 meters in the football field is converted as follows:

$$91.44 \text{ meters } *1/1000 \ ^{meter}/_{centimeters} = 0.09144 \text{ kilometers}$$

Meters, kilometers, centimeters are commonly used metric units. The other commonly used unit is the millimeter. Since the Prefix "milli" means "one thousandth", we are readily able to convert using powers of ten.

Can you see that there are ten millimeters in one centimeter? Can you also see that there are 1000 times 1000 millimeters in one kilometer? That means that a millimeter (close to one thirty second of an inch) is about one millionth of a kilometer.

WRITING

Expanding Your Vocabulary

The organic way to expand your vocabulary is to read everything you can get your hands on. That means blogs, articles and social media, but also physical books, posted signs and even the labels on your shampoo bottle. Start looking for opportunities to read a little bit more every day, from now until the day of the test.

Of course, you do have that test coming up, so you don't have much time to go au naturale. We got your back. Here is your first and most crucial vocabulary hack: identifying root words.

What is the What?

Many words are little stories in and of themselves, which is to say that they have a beginning, middle and end. These parts are, respectively, the prefix, the root word and the suffix.

Not all words have all three parts. Sometimes it's just the prefix and root, sometimes just the root and suffix, and sometimes there are multiple roots. But—and this is important—a word is never made up only of prefixes and suffixes. There is always at least one root word, because that's the main idea of the word. You can't have a complete, grammatically correct sentence without a subject, and you can't have a complete word without a main idea, or root word.

For example, here's a word that's close to your heart lately: *reviewing.* It means viewing something again. Here are its parts:
Prefix = re
Root = view
Suffix = ing

Re is a prefix that basically means again. *View* means *see* or look. *Ing* is a suffix that tells you the root word is happening. So, if you're reviewing, you're viewing something again. Thus, the root word, or main idea, is view.

Let's get concrete: If you went up to one of your friends and just said, "Again," they would give you a funny look and say, "What again?"

It's the same idea if you went up to them and said, "Doing." They would say, "Doing what?"

If you went up to them and just said, "Look," they would look where you're looking to determine what you're seeing. They may not know what to look for, but they get the idea.

Almost every vocabulary word on the test will be some combination of prefixes, roots and suffixes. If you run into one that you don't know, the first question to ask yourself is, "What is the what?"

Here is another example: *unemployment*
Prefix = un
Root = employ

Suffix = ment

You can't just say "un" or "ment" and expect to be understood, but when you add the main idea, *employ*, the word makes sense. It means the state of not having a job.

Where It Gets Messy

Of course, we speak the English language, which is a marvelous, madcap collage of many other languages, but mostly Latin, German and Greek. That means many root words are not English words. On top of that, there are no hard-and-fast rules for how prefixes and suffixes will change root words, so each root may look a little different depending on which prefixes and suffixes are used.

However, you can usually get the gist by breaking off the parts that you know are prefixes and suffixes and asking yourself what the remaining part reminds you of.

In order to break things down, you need to have a grasp of the most common prefixes, suffixes and root words you'll encounter on the test (these are outlined below).

Prefixes
Here are your opposite prefixes, which you'll encounter a lot on the test:

Prefix	Variations	What it Means	Examples
Anti-	Ant-	Against or opposite	Anti-inflammatory, antagonist
De-		Opposite	Decontaminate, deconstruct
Dis-		Not or opposite	Disagree, dis (slang for insult)
In-	Im-, Il-, Ir-	Not	Incapable, impossible, illegitimate, irreplaceable
Non-		Not	Noncompliant, nonsense
Un-		Not	Unfair, unjust

Here is a quick list of some other common prefixes:

Prefix	Variations	What it Means	Examples
En-	Em-	Cause	Enlighten, empower
Fore-		Before	Foresee, foretell
In-		Inside of	Inland, income
Inter-		Between	Interrupt, interaction
Mid-		In the middle of	Midair, midlife
Mis-		Wrong	Mistake, misdiagnose
Pre-		Before	Pregame, prefix
Re-		Again	Review, recompress
Semi-		Half or partial	Semitruck, semiannual
Sub-		Under	Subconscious, subpar
Super-		Above	Superimpose, superstar
Trans-		Across	Translate, transform

Suffixes

Here are some common suffixes you'll encounter on the test:

Suffix	Variations	What it Means	Examples
-Able	-Ible	Can be accomplished	Capable, possible
-Al	-Ial	Has traits of	Additional, beneficial
-En		Made of	Molten, wooden
-Er		More than	Luckier, richer
-Er	-Or	Agent that does	Mover, actor
-Est		Most	Largest, happiest
-Ic		Has traits of	Acidic, dynamic
-Ing		Continues to do	Reviewing, happening
-Ion	-Tion, -Ation, -Ition	Process of	Occasion, motion, rotation, condition
-Ity		The state of	Ability, simplicity
-Ly		Has traits of	Friendly, kindly
-Ment		Process/state of	Enlightenment, establishment
-Ness		State of	Happiness, easiness
-Ous	-Eous, -Ious	Has traits of	Porous, gaseous, conscious
-Y		Has traits of	Artsy, fartsy

Common Root Words

If you can't identify a word because it seems like it's in another language, that's most likely because it is. This isn't always true, but a good general rule is that our longer, more academic words tend to have their roots in Latin and Greek, while our shorter words tend to have their roots in German. For example, *amorous* and *loving* are synonyms, but one has its roots in the Latin *amor* and the other in the German *lieb*.

Latin/Greek

Because vocabulary words on the test tend toward the longer, more academic variety, you'll get the most out of studying some common Latin and Greek roots:

Root	Variations	What it Means	Examples
Aster	Astro	Star	Astronomy, disaster
Aqua		Water	Aquatic, aquarium
Aud		Hear	Auditorium, audience
Bene		Good	Benevolent, benign
Bio		Life	Biology, autobiography
Cent		Hundred	Century, cent (money)
Chrono		Time	Chronological, synchronize
Circum	Circa	Around	Circumspect, circumnavigate
Contra	Counter	Against or conflict	Contraband, encounter
Dict		Speak or say	Dictate, dictation
Duc	Duct, duce	Lead or leader	Produce, conduct
Fac		Make or do	Manufacture, facsimile (fax)
Fract	Frag	Break	Fraction, defragment
Gen		Birth or create	Genetics, generate
Graph		Write	Telegraph, calligraphy
Ject		Throw	Inject, projection
Jur	Jus	Law	Juror, justice
Log	Logue	Concept or thought	Logo, dialogue
Mal		Bad	Maladaptive, malevolent
Man		Hand	Manuscript, manual
Mater		Mother	Maternal, material
Mis	Mit	Send	Mission, submit
Pater	Pat	Father	Paternal, patriot
Path		Feel	Sympathy, empathetic
Phile	Philo	Love	Philosophy, anglophile
Phon		Sound	Telephone, phonetic
Photo		Light	Photograph, photosynthesis
Port		Carry	Transport, portable
Psych	Psycho	Soul or spirit	Psychiatrist, psyche
Qui	Quit	Quiet or rest	Acquittal, tranquility
Rupt		Break	Rupture, interrupt
Scope		See, inspect	Telescope, microscopic
Scrib	Script	Write	Describe, transcription
Sens	Sent	Feel	Sensory, consent
Spect		Look	Spectate, circumspect
Struct		Build	Construct, obstruction
Techno	Tech	Art or science	Technical, technology
Tele		Far	Teleport, television
Therm		Heat	Thermometer, thermal
Vac		Empty	Vacation, evacuate
Vis	Vid	See	Visual, video
Voc		Speak or call	Vocal, vocation

Vocabulary Practice Test

For items 1-5, try to identify the root and write an English translation or synonym for it. We did the first one for you as an example.

#	Word	Root	Translation/Synonym
Ex	Description	Script	Something written
1	Irresponsible		
2	Entombment		
3	Professorial		
4	Unconscionable		
5	Gainfully		

For items 6-10, identify the prefix and write an English translation or synonym for it.

#	Word	Prefix	Translation/Synonym
Ex	Prepare	Pre	Before
6	Proceed		
7	Misapprehend		
8	Antibiotic		
9	Hyperactive		
10	Cacophony		

For items 11-15, identify the suffix and write an English translation or synonym for it.

#	Word	Suffix	Translation/Synonym
Ex	Lovable	Able	Can be accomplished
11	Tedious		
12	Absolution		
13	Cathartic		
14	Merriment		
15	Inspector		

Now, it's time to test your current vocabulary:

1. Achromatic most nearly means:
a. full of color
b. fragrant
c. without color
d. vivid

2. Cursory most nearly means:
a. meticulous; careful
b. undetailed; rapid
c. thorough
d. expletive

3. Hearsay most nearly means:
a. blasphemy
b. secondhand information that can't be proven
c. evidence that can be confirmed
d. testimony

4. Magnanimous most nearly means:
a. suspicious
b. uncontested
c. forgiving; not petty
d. stingy; cheap

5. Terrestrial most nearly means:
a. of the earth
b. cosmic
c. otherworldly/unearthly
d. supernatural

Let's see how you did:

1. c. without color
2. b. undetailed; rapid
3. b. secondhand information that can't be proven
4. c. forgiving; not petty
5. a. of the earth

Words in Context

When reading through a chapter in a book or a passage on a test, you will sometimes encounter a word you've never seen before. You may not know what it means, but don't worry! You can still figure out a basic definition of the word, even if you don't have a dictionary in hand (or if you don't want to get off the sofa and get one).

In every sentence, any given word is surrounded by clauses, phrases and other words. When you find a word you don't recognize, you can learn more about it by studying the context surrounding it. These surrounding words, phrases and clauses are called context clues. Using these, you can determine the definition for almost every unfamiliar word you encounter. This is a skill that will become especially helpful when you start reading higher-level texts with fancy words or training manuals with lots of jargon.

Types of Context Clues
As you read, you can use several different types of context clues to help you discover the meaning of unknown words. Some important and common types of context clues are outlined below. Try to use the specific context clue to determine the meaning of the bolded word.

Root Word & Affix
This is a context clue that uses your existing knowledge of common root words.

Example: Scientists who dig up dinosaur bones are experts in **paleontology**.

This context clue assumes you have knowledge of dinosaurs and can relate that to the study of "paleontology."

Compare/Contrast
This is a context clue that signals a similarity or difference by using words or phrases that denote a comparison or contrast. Words that imply similarity (or comparison) include *like, also, just as, too,* etc. Words that imply difference (or contrast) include *whereas, opposed to, unlike, versus,* etc.

Example: A comet, like an **asteroid**, is made from leftover matter in the universe.

This context clue compares an "asteroid" with a comet to imply a similarity to the given definition of a comet.

Logic
This is a context clue wherein you must infer the definition of the unknown word by using the relationships within the sentence.

Example: Builders routinely use **fasteners** that will help hold their structures and buildings in place.

This context clue describes the job that "fasteners" do.
Definition

This is a context clue that includes a basic definition of the unknown word.

Example: New biological species can be formed through a process called **speciation**.

This context clue defines "speciation" outright.

Example or Illustration

This is a context clue that uses an example or illustration of the unknown word.

Example: Animals classified in the phylum porifera live in a **marine** habitat like the Atlantic and Pacific Oceans.

This context clue uses Atlantic and Pacific Oceans as examples of "marine" habitats.

Homographs

Now that you've had a refresher on context clues, let's talk about homographs. A homograph is a word that is spelled exactly like another word, but has a different meaning. For example, "bass" can mean "a low, deep sound" or "a type of fish." Here's a more complex homograph: "minute" can mean "a unit of time" or "something very small."

Although questions with homographs aren't necessarily difficult, you'll need to pay extra attention to the context clues. If you're rushing or don't read the entire sentence, you can accidentally mark an incorrect answer by mistaking the homograph for the wrong meaning. As long as you take your time and use the context clues, you'll most likely have no problem.

Here's something to consider when you take the exam. Within the question, replace the vocabulary term with your selected answer choice. Read the sentence and check whether or not it makes sense. This won't guarantee a correct answer, but it will help identify an incorrect one.

Another point to keep in mind is that sometimes there will not be an answer choice that exactly fits into the sentence. Don't panic! You probably did not misread the context clues or come up with an incorrect meaning. Many times, questions will ask you to select the *best* word from the given answer choices, even though that correct answer choice may not be the best *possible* answer overall. These types of questions want you to choose the *most* correct answer choice. These can be tricky to tackle, but expect to see questions like this on the exam. Just remember the tip above and you'll do fine.

Vocabulary-in-Context

Vocabulary-in-Context questions ask you for the definition of a word as it is used within the context of the passage. The format of these questions is similar to that of Word Knowledge questions. You will be given a word and asked to select the closest meaning from a list of four choices. The difference, though, is that where Word Knowledge questions test straightforward vocabulary, the words chosen for Vocabulary-in-context questions are often words that can have more than one meaning. You will need to use context clues from the passage in order to figure out which meaning is correct.

It's also important to note that many questions on the exam will not always ask you to simply determine the meaning of a vocabulary word. Many times, instead of asking you for a synonym or definition of a vocabulary word, the question will ask you what the vocabulary word "most nearly means". For these types of questions, you'll need to use context clues and your existing vocabulary knowledge to determine which answer choice has a meaning that is closest to that of the vocabulary word.

To answer these questions, reread the sentence from the passage that the word is taken from. Come up with a prediction—your own definition or synonym of what the word means as used in that sentence. Then, look at the answer choices and choose the one that best matches your prediction. If you do not see your prediction among the answer choices, read each of the answer choices as part of the sentence, replacing the original word, and choose the one that makes the most sense.

Let's look at some examples.

Some of the questions you'll encounter will ask you to fill in the blank in a sentence. For the questions below, select the word that fits best in the sentence.

1. The bolt was _____. It took a lot of effort to loosen the fastener.
A. Rusted
B. Shiny
C. Loose
D. Strong

Answer: A.
Using the context clues in the sentence, you can assume that the missing word is somehow related to the phrase "loosen the fastener". Something about the bolt made it difficult to remove. You can immediately eliminate "shiny" since it is not related to the action of removing a fastener. Likewise, "loose" is not correct because if the bolt were loose, it wouldn't be difficult to remove it. "Strong" could possibly fit if there wasn't a better answer choice, but it's not typically used to describe how difficult a fastener is to remove. The word that best fits in the sentence is "rusted" because rust directly increases the difficulty of removing a fastener.

2. As the commanding officer's eyes widened and his face turned red, he proceeded to _____ the lance corporal.

A. Tease

B. Scold

C. Compliment

D. Correct

Answer: B.

Using the context clues in the sentence, you can assume that the missing word is somehow linked to widened eyes and a red face, which are associated with anger. You can immediately eliminate "tease" and "compliment" since those words connote lightheartedness and sincerity, not exactly similar to the demeanor described in the sentence. "Correct" could possibly fit if there wasn't a better answer choice, but it's not necessarily associated with widened eyes and a red face. The word that best fits in the sentence is "scold" because scolding connotes anger or irritation, which correlate with widened eyes and a red face.

Sure, those were fairly easy, but those are just one type of vocabulary-in-context questions you'll probably encounter on the exam. For the questions below, select the word that MOST NEARLY means the same as the underlined word.

1. The chairman of the board <u>abandoned</u> his position after a damaging scandal.

A. Squandered

B. Resigned

C. Ignored

D. Neglected

Answer: B.

All the answer choices connote negative characteristics of the position of chairman of the board, but only "resigned" most closely matches the underlined word. "Squandered" suggests a wasted opportunity. "Ignored" means deliberately taking no notice of. "Neglected" signifies a failure to pay attention to. "Resigned" indicates voluntarily leaving a job, which MOST nearly means the same as "abandoned", leaving permanently.

2. Sarah considered herself a <u>parsimonious</u> shopper. She loved finding great shopping deals.

A. Cheap

B. Frugal

C. Economical

D. Thrifty

Answer: A.

All the answer choices reflect the general meaning of "parsimonious", being careful with money, but only one choice has a negative association. "Frugal", "economical" and "thrifty" are all adjectives with a positive connotation, but "cheap" is usually used as a negative description.

Those were a bit more difficult, but let's try a few more. For the questions below, select the word that LEAST LIKELY means the same as the underlined word.

1. The evidence of the murder was <u>destroyed</u> before the trial.
A. Devastated
B. Obliterated
C. Ruined
D. Incinerated

Answer: D.
While all the answer choices can be used in place of "destroyed", "incinerated" suggests a specific type of damage: destruction by fire. Technically, "incinerated" is a logical answer, but the question isn't asking which choice is not logical. It's asking which choice LEAST likely means the underlined word. This was a tough one, but you should expect to see some questions like this on the exam.

2. While trying to negotiate a peace treaty, one side was being entirely <u>hostile</u> to the other.
A. Belligerent
B. Threatening
C. Averse
D. Combative

Answer: C.
While all the choices are mostly synonyms of "hostile", only one choice excludes a violent implication in its definition. "Averse" means strongly opposed to, but "belligerent", "threatening" and "combative" all suggest harm or death, as does "hostile".

Sometimes, you will need to read a passage before answering the questions. Let's look at some examples of those questions.

"American elections consist of citizens voting for their government representatives. Today, this includes members of the U.S. Senate, but this was not always the case. When the United States Constitution was first written, the people did not get to elect their senators directly. Instead, the senators were appointed by state legislators (who are elected directly by the people in their respective states). This changed in 1913, however, with the 17th Amendment to the Constitution. This amendment allows for the direct election of U.S. Senators by the citizenry. While this election process can make the senators more accountable to their constituents, since the citizens will decide whether a senator will keep his or her job at the next election, it diminishes the voice that state legislatures have in the federal government."

1. The word <u>constituents</u> in the passage most nearly means:
A. Elements
B. Employees
C. Senators
D. Voters

Answer: D.
By reading the choices back into the sentence, you can see that the best synonym for "constituents" is "voters". It is the voters who decide whether or not to reelect the senators. The word "constituents" on its own can have several meanings, including voters, elements, members, components and parts. In the context of this passage, however, "voters" is the best definition.

2. The word <u>amendment</u> in the passage most nearly means:
A. Rule
B. Principle
C. Alteration
D. Truth

Answer: C.

By reading the choices back into the sentence, you can see that the best synonym for "amendment" is "alteration". The passage states how the Constitution originally provided for senator selection. However, the passage explains the difference in process after the 17th amendment. Because "alteration" means "change", it is the best choice.

READING PRACTICE TEST

Passage 1

The United States Treasury operates a subsidiary, the Bureau of Engraving and Printing (BEP), where the nation's supply of paper money is designed and manufactured. But to call American currency "paper" money is a slight misnomer that understates its unperceived complexity and intrinsic technological sophistication. The Treasury goes to extraordinary lengths to safeguard cash from counterfeiters. One of the most fundamental ways is by printing not on paper, per se, but on a proprietary blend of linen and cotton. American money is more akin to fabric than paper, and each bill that is printed is a phenomenal work of art and masterful craftsmanship.

The most frequently counterfeited denominations are the 20-dollar bill, preferred by domestic counterfeiters, and the 100-dollar note, which is the currency of choice for foreign forgers. To make the copying of twenties more difficult, the BEP uses color-shifting ink that changes from copper to green in certain lights. Evidence of this can be seen in the numeral "20" located in the lower right corner on the front of the bills. A portrait watermark – which is a very faint, rather ethereal image of President Jackson – is also juxtaposed into the blank space to the right to his visible and prominent portrait. Additionally, there is a security ribbon, adorned with a flag and the words "USA Twenty," printed on and embedded into the bill. When exposed to ultraviolet light, the thread glows with a greenish hue. Twenties also include an almost subliminal text that reads "USA20;" this micro-printed text is well-camouflaged within the bill. With the use of a magnifying glass, it can be found in the border beneath the Treasurer's signature.

The 100-dollar bill utilizes similar security features. These include color-shifting ink, portrait watermarks, security threads and ribbons, raised printing, and micro-printing. These units of currency, dubbed "Ben Franklins" in honor of the president whose face graces it, also boast what the BEP describes as a 3-D security ribbon. The ribbon has bells and numbers printed on it. When the currency is tilted it appears that the images of bells transform into the numeral 100 and, when tilted side to side, the bells and 100s seem to move in a lateral direction.

Security threads woven into each different denomination have their own respective colors, and each one glows a different color when illuminated with ultraviolet light. Fine engraving or printing patterns appear in various locations on bills too, and many of these patterns are extremely fine. The artists who create them for engraving also incorporate non-linear designs, as the waviness can make it exponentially more difficult to successfully counterfeit the currency. The surface of American currency is also slightly raised, giving it a subtly, but distinct, tactile characteristic.

1. Which of the following conclusions may logically be drawn from the first paragraph of the passage?
   a) Linen and cotton are more expensive printing materials than paper.
   b) The current process of printing money is reflective of decades of modifications.
   c) Counterfeiting of American money is an enormous problem.
   d) The artistry inherent in the making of American money makes it attractive to collectors.

2. What sentence, if added to the end of the passage, would provide the best conclusion to both the paragraph and the passage?
   a) It is clear from all these subtly nuanced features of the various bills that true artistry is at work in their making.
   b) Yet, despite all of these technological innovations, the race to stay ahead of savvy counterfeiters and their constantly changing counterfeiting techniques is a never- ending one.
   c) Due to the complexities involved in the printing of money, these artists are consequently well-paid for their skills.
   d) Thus, many other countries have begun to model their money-printing methods on these effective techniques.

3. The passage is reflective of which of the following types of writing?
   a) Descriptive
   b) Narrative
   c) Expository
   d) Persuasive

4. This passage likely comes from which of the following documents?
   a) A pamphlet for tourists visiting the United States Treasury
   b) A feature news article commemorating the bicentennial of the Bureau of Engraving and Printing
   c) A letter from the US treasury Secretary to the President
   d) A public service message warning citizens about the increased circulation of counterfeit currency

5. Which of the following is an example of a primary source document?
   a) A pamphlet for tourists visiting the United States Treasury
   b) A feature news article commemorating the bicentennial of the Bureau of Engraving and Printing
   c) A letter from the US treasury Secretary to the President
   d) A public service message warning citizens about the increased circulation of counterfeit currency

6. Which of the following describes the word intrinsic as it is used in the first paragraph of the passage?
   a) Amazing
   b) Expensive
   c) Unbelievable
   d) Inherent

Passage 2
In the Middle Ages, merchants an artisans formed groups called "guilds" to protect themselves and their trades. Guilds appeared in the year 1000, and by the twelfth century, analogous trades, like wool, spice, and silk dealers had formed their own guilds.
_____ , towns like Florence, Italy, boasted as many as 50 merchants' guilds. With the advent of guilds, apprenticeship became a complex system. Apprentices were to be taught only certain things and then they were to prove they possessed certain skills, as determined by the guild. Each guild decided the length of time required for an apprentice to work for a master tradesman before being admitted to the trade.

7. The topic sentence of the above passage is
   a) In the Middle Ages, merchants an artisans formed groups called "guilds" to protect themselves and their trades.
   b) Guilds appeared in the year 1000, and by the twelfth century, analogous trades, like wool, spice, and silk dealers had formed their own guilds.
   c) With the advent of guilds, apprenticeship became a complex system.
   d) Apprentices were to be taught only certain things and then they were to prove they possessed certain skills, as determined by the guild.

8. The main idea of the passage is that
   a) wool, spice and silk dealers were all types of merchant trades during the Middle Ages.
   b) Florence, Italy was a great center of commerce during the Middle Ages.
   c) merchant guilds originated in the Middle Ages and became extremely popular, eventually leading to a sophisticated apprenticeship system.
   d) apprenticeships were highly sought after, therefore merchants had many skilled workers to choose from to assist them in their trade.

9. From the content of the passage, it reasonably be inferred that
   a) prior to the inception of guilds, merchants were susceptible to competition from lesser skilled craftsmen peddling inferior products or services.
   b) most merchants were unscrupulous business who often cheated their customers.
   c) it was quite easy to become an apprentice to a highly skilled merchant.
   d) guilds fell out of practice during the Industrial Revolution due to the mechanization of labor.

10. As it is used in the second sentence, "analogous" most nearly means
    a) obsolete
    b) inferior
    c) similar
    d) less popular

11. Which of the following is the best signal word or phrase to fill in the blank above?
    a) Up until that time,
    b) Before that time,
    c) By that time,
    d) After that time,

Passage 3
Certainly we must face this fact: if the American press, as a mass medium, has formed the minds of America, the mass has also formed the medium. There is action, reaction, and interaction going on ceaselessly between the newspaper-buying public and the editors. What is wrong with the American press is what is in part wrong with American society. Is this,_____, to exonerate the American press for its failures to give the American people more tasteful and more illuminating reading matter? Can the American press seek to be excused from responsibility for public lack of information as TV and radio often do, on the grounds that, after all, "we have to give the people what they want or we will go out of business"?
--Clare Boothe Luce

12. What is the primary purpose of this text?
    a) To reveal an innate problem in American society
    b) To criticize the American press for not taking responsibility for their actions
    c) To analyze the complex relationship that exists between the public and the media
    d) To challenge the masses to protest the lack of information disseminated by the media

13. From which of the following is the above paragraph most likely excerpted?
    a) A newspaper editorial letter
    b) A novel about yellow journalism
    c) A diary entry
    d) A speech given at a civil rights protest

14. Which of the following is an example of a primary source document?
    a) A newspaper editorial letter
    b) A novel about yellow journalism
    c) A diary entry
    d) A speech given at a civil rights protest

15. As it is used in sentence 4, "illuminating" most nearly means
    a) intelligent
    b) sophisticated
    c) interesting
    d) enlightening

16. Which of the following is the best signal word or phrase to fill in the blank?
    a) so
    b) however
    c) therefore
    d) yet

17. What is the author's primary attitude towards the American press?
    a) admiration
    b) perplexity
    c) disapproval
    d) ambivalence

18. Which of the following identifies the mode of the passage?
    a) expository
    b) persuasive/argumentative
    c) narrative
    d) descriptive

19. Based on the passage, which of the following can most likely be concluded?
    a) The author has a degree in journalism
    b) The author has worked in the journalism industry
    c) The author is seeking employment at a newspaper
    d) The author is filing a lawsuit against a media outlet

Passage 4

The game today known as "football" in the United States can be traced directly back to the English game of rugby, although there have been many changes to the game. Football was played informally on university fields more than a hundred years ago. In 1840, a yearly series of informal "scrimmages" started at Yale University. It took more than twenty-five years,_____, for the game to become a part of college life. The first formal intercollegiate football game was held between Princeton and Rutgers teams on November 6, 1869 on Rutgers' home field at New Brunswick, New Jersey, and Rutgers won.

20. Which sentence, if added to the end of the paragraph, would provide the best conclusion?
   a) Despite an invitation to join the Ivy League, Rutgers University declined, but later joined the Big Ten Conference instead.
   b) Football was played for decades on school campuses nationwide before the American Professional Football Association was formed in 1920, and then renamed the National Football League (or the NFL) two years later.
   c) Women were never allowed to play football, and that fact remains a controversial policy at many colleges and universities.
   d) Football remains the national pastime, despite rising popularity for the game of soccer, due to increased TV coverage of World Cup matches.

21. Which of the following is the best signal word or phrase to fill in the blank above?
   a) however
   b) still
   c) in addition
   d) alternatively

Passage 5

Modernism is a philosophical movement that arose during the early 20th century. Among the factors that shaped modernism were the development of modern societies based on industry and the rapid growth of cities, followed later by the horror of World War I. Modernism rejected the science-based thinking of the earlier Era of Enlightenment, and many modernists also rejected religion. The poet Ezra Pound's 1934 injunction to "Make it new!" was the touchstone of the movement's approach towards what it saw as the now obsolete culture of the past. A notable characteristic of modernism is self-consciousness and irony concerning established literary and social traditions, which often led to experiments concerned with HOW things were made, not so much with the actual final product. Modernism had a profound impact on numerous aspects of life, and its values and perspectives still influence society in many positive ways today.

22. According to the passage, what is the overarching theme of the modernist movement?
   a) Rejection of the past and outmoded ideas
   b) Appreciation of urban settings over natural settings
   c) A concentration on method over form
   d) A focus on automated industry

23. As it is used in the passage, "touchstone" most nearly means
   a) Challenge
   b) Basis
   c) Fashion
   d) Metaphor

24. Which of the following statements from the passage can be described as an opinion?
    a) Among the factors that shaped modernism were the development of modern societies based on industry and the rapid growth of cities, followed later by the horror of World War I.
    b) The poet Ezra Pound's 1934 injunction to "Make it new!" was the touchstone of the movement's approach towards what it saw as the now obsolete culture of the past.
    c) A notable characteristic of modernism is self-consciousness and irony concerning established literary and social traditions, which often led to experiments concerned with HOW things were made, not so much with the actual final product.
    d) Modernism had a profound impact on numerous aspects of life, and its values and perspectives still influence society in many positive ways today.

Passage 6
The modern Olympics are the leading international sporting event featuring summer and winter sports competitions in which thousands of athletes from around the world participate in a variety of competitions. Held every two years, with the Summer and Winter Games alternating, the games are a modern way to bring nations together,_____ allowing for national pride, and sportsmanship on a global scale. Having withstood the test of time over many centuries, they are the best example of the physical achievements of mankind.

The creation of the modern Games was inspired by the ancient Olympic Games, which were held in Olympia, Greece, from the 8th century BC to the 4th century AD. The Ancient Games events were fewer in number and were examples of very basic traditional forms of competitive athleticism. Many running events were featured, as well as a pentathlon (consisting of a jumping event, discus and javelin throws, a foot race, and wrestling), boxing, wrestling, pankration, and equestrian events. Fast forward to the modern state of this ancient athletic competition, and we see that the Olympic Movement during the 20th and 21st centuries has resulted in several changes to the Games, including the creation of the Winter Olympic Games for ice and winter sports, which for climate reasons, would not have been possible in ancient Greece. The Olympics has also shifted away from pure amateurism to allowing participation of professional athletes, a change which was met with criticism when first introduced, as many felt it detracted from the original spirit and intention of the competition.

Today, over 13,000 athletes compete at the summer and Winter Olympic Games in 33 different sports and nearly 400 events. The first, second, and third-place finishers in each event receive Olympic medals: gold, silver, and bronze, respectively. And every country hopes to be able to go home with many of these medals, as they are truly still a point of pride for each nation to be recognized for some outstanding achievement on the world stage, however briefly.

25. Which of the following is the best signal word or phrase to fill in the blank in the first paragraph?
    a) despite
    b) however
    c) instead of
    d) as well as

26. Which of the following words from the last sentence of paragraph 2 has a negative connotation?
    a) Shifted
    b) Allowing
    c) Change
    d) Detracted

27. Which of the following statements based on the passage would be considered an opinion?
   a) The ancient Olympic games were held in Olympia, Greece.
   b) The Olympic games are the best example of humanity's physical prowess.
   c) When the games were changed from pure amateurism to allowing professional athletes to participate, this change displeased many people.
   d) Today, 33 different sports are represented at the Olympic games.

Passage 7
A day or two later, in the afternoon, I saw myself staring at my fire, at an inn which I had booked on foreseeing that I would spend some weeks in London. I had just come in, and, having decided on a spot for my luggage, sat down to consider my room. It was on the ground floor, and the fading daylight reached it in a sadly broken-down condition. It struck me that the room was stuffy and unsocial, with its moldy smell and its decoration of lithographs and waxy flowers
– it seemed an impersonal black hole in the huge general blackness of the inn itself. The uproar of the neighborhood outside hummed away, and the rattle of a heartless hansom cab passed close to my ears. A sudden horror of the whole place came over me, like a tiger-pounce of homesickness which had been watching its moment. London seemed hideous, vicious, cruel and, above all, overwhelming. Soon, I would have to go out for my dinner, and it appeared to me that I would rather remain dinnerless, would rather even starve, than go forth into the hellish town where a stranger might get trampled to death, and have his carcass thrown into the Thames River.

28. Based on the passage above, the author's attitude toward his experience in London can best be described as:
   a) Awe
   b) Disappointment
   c) Revulsion
   d) Ambivalence

29. Which type of document is this passage likely excerpted from?
   a) A travel guide
   b) A diary entry
   c) A news editorial
   d) An advertisement

30. Which of the following documents would likely NOT be considered a primary source document?
   a) A travel guide
   b) A diary entry
   c) A news editorial
   d) An advertisement

31. Based on the content of the passage, which of the following is a reasonable conclusion?
   a) The author is quite wealthy.
   b) The author has been to London before.
   c) The author is traveling to London based on the recommendation of a friend.
   d) The author will not be traveling to London again.

Reading Practice Test – Answer Key

1.   C. Counterfeiting of American money is an enormous problem.
Rationale: C is the best option as we are told that "The Treasury goes to extraordinary lengths to safeguard cash from counterfeiters."

2.   B. Yet, despite all of these technological innovations, the race to stay ahead of savvy counterfeiters and their constantly changing counterfeiting techniques is a never- ending one.
Rationale: B is the best as the main point of the passage is to emphasize the extent of counterfeiting and detail the technology used to counteract such constantly changing fraudulent activity.

3.   C. Expository
Rationale: C. An expository essay is one in which an idea is investigated and expounded upon, and an argument is set forth presenting evidence concerning that idea in a clear and concise manner. In this case the idea being investigated and expounded upon is anti- counterfeiting techniques.

4.   A. A pamphlet for tourists visiting the United States Treasury
Rationale: A. The style and specific subject matter all indicate that it is most likely from an informational pamphlet written for visitors to the Bureau of Engraving and Printing.

5.   C. A letter from the US treasury Secretary to the President
Rationale: C. A primary source document is one which was created and serves as a first- hand source of information or evidence about a particular time period. Only the personal letter would meet the criteria of a primary source.

6.   D. Inherent
Rationale: D. Technological sophistication is inherent, (or naturally found) in the making of American money, so much so that to call it "paper" does not fully reveal how complex a product it really is.

7.   A. In the Middle Ages, merchants an artisans formed groups called "guilds" to protect themselves and their trades.
Rationale: A. The first sentence is the topic sentence because it introduces the main idea of the paragraph.

8.   C. merchant guilds originated in the Middle Ages and became extremely popular, eventually leading to a sophisticated apprenticeship system.
Rationale: C. The guild system's origins and development is the main idea of the paragraph. The other options are too narrow to constitute a main idea.

9.   A. prior to the inception of guilds, merchants were susceptible to competition from lesser skilled craftsmen peddling inferior products or services.
Rationale: A. It can be inferred that if guilds were instituted, there must have been a need for merchants to safeguard themselves from threats to their livelihood.

10.   C. similar
Rationale: C. The sentence conveys to us that the spice, silk and wool dealers were similar tradesman to that of other merchants who had set up guilds.

11.   C. By that time,

Rationale: C. The passage introduces the inception of guilds and their development over time, chronologically. From the previous sentence, it is clear that guilds grew in popularity over the centuries, until towns like Florence had 50 guilds by the twelfth century. "By that time" most clearly states this increase and development over time.

12.   B. To criticize the American press for not taking responsibility for their actions Rationale: B. Luce is clearly criticizing the press for not taking responsibility to disseminate enlightening information to the public, and instead are blaming the public for not asking for reading matter which is "tasteful and more illuminating".

13.   A. A newspaper editorial letter
Rationale: A. Given the paragraph's opinionated style and serious, critical tone, it most likely excerpted from a longer letter printed in the op/ed section of a newspaper.

14.   C. A diary entry
Rationale: C. The diary entry (which would likely provide firsthand thoughts, feelings and opinions about current life or world events as witnessed by the author) would qualify as a primary source document of evidence or information of a particular time period.

15.   D. enlightening
Rationale: D. Illuminating reading matter is that which would be enlightening and provide necessary information to the public.

16.   C. therefore
Rationale: C. Luce is using a cause and effect argument here, but she is questioning the excuse of the press to not do their job as a result of certain demands of the public, which would "therefore exonerate the American press for its failures to give the American people more tasteful and more illuminating reading matter".

17.   C. disapproval
Rationale: C. Luce clearly disapproves of the press and their practice of serving up a lack of news to the public, "on the grounds that, after all, "[they] have to give the people what they want or [they] will go out of business".

18.   B. persuasive/argumentative
Rationale: B. Luce utilizes several modes of writing here, but overall, she is critical of the American press, and is arguing that they are at fault for not giving the American public useful information or "illuminating reading matter".

19.   B. The author has worked in the journalism industry
Rationale: B. The author clearly has an understanding of the business of the media, as well as its public responsibility to inform citizens, so it can be concluded that she likely has worked in the journalism industry. None of the other statements can reasonably be concluded based on the content of the passage.

20.   B. Football was played for decades on school campuses nationwide before the American Professional Football Association was formed in 1920, and then renamed the National Football League (or the NFL) two years later.
Rationale: B. This statement adds additional information to the paragraph about the progression of the game of football in the US and therefore, appropriately concludes the paragraph. The other statements discuss topics not directly related to football, or add additional information that is slightly off topic.

21.   A. however
Rationale: A. The sentence is explaining that, despite the appearance of football as a sport on some college campuses, and annual scrimmages occurring at Yale, 25 years passed before it became a regular activity in college life. "However" shows this contrast best.

22.   A. Rejection of the past and outmoded ideas
Rationale: A. From the paragraph it is clear that modernism is mainly concerned with rejecting the ideas of the past -- like the science of the enlightenment, and old ideas about religion –and instead focusing on creating what was "New".

23.   B. Basis
Rationale: Pound's suggestion to "Make it new" was the basis, or touchstone of the Modernist movement's outlook and approach to interpreting the world and society.

24.   D. Modernism had a profound impact on numerous aspects of life, and its values and perspectives still influence society in many positive ways today.
Rationale: D. The author's description of Modernism's influence as being "positive" is clearly an opinion about the nature of the influence. The other statements are factually based, providing general information about the Modernist movement.

25.   D. as well as
Rationale: D. This sentence discusses all of the positive benefits that result from the continuation of the Olympic games in the present day, so "as well as" is the correct signal phrase to convey this idea, in a list form.

26.   D. Detracted
Rationale: D. The idea that allowing professional athletes to participate in the games would cause people to believe it "detracted" from the intentions of the original, is a negative notion, as it suggests that this would take away from the games, instead of adding something positive.

27.   B. The Olympic games are the best example of humanity's physical prowess. Rationale: B. This statement is the opinion of the author, as there is no indication that this idea has been tested or proven in any way, but is simply what the author believes or feels.

28.   C. Revulsion
Rationale: C. The author uses words like "moldy smell" and "black hole" to describe his rented room in the inn, and "heartless" and "hideous" to describe the environment of London, adding that he "would rather even starve" than go out to find himself a meal in the "hellish town where a stranger might get trampled to death". These are very strong negative sentiments that clearly indicate his revulsion to the city.

29.   B. A diary entry
Rationale: B. The personal and frank tone that the author uses to describe his hotel room and his private fears about going out into the city of London for dinner suggest that this would have been written in a journal or diary.

30.   D. An advertisement
Rationale: D. A primary source document is one which was created from first-hand experience under a period of study of a particular event, moment in time, situation etc. A travel guide, diary entry and news editorial could all potentially be primary sources which chronicle one of the aforementioned. The only one that would likely NOT qualify as a primary source is the advertisement, as usually advertisements are meant to persuade

one to engage in an experience, purchase a product or the like, and are often not completely based in personal experience and may not even be factual.

31.   D. The author will not be traveling to London again.
Rationale: D. It is clear that the author is unhappy with his lodging and finds London a generally disagreeable place, so it is likely that he would not travel to London again. The other statements are not reasonable conclusions which can be made from the content of the passage.

MATHEMATICS PRACTICE TEST

1. Change to an improper fraction: 2 1/3
    a) 5/3
    b) 3/7
    c) 7/3
    d) 8/3

2. Which of the following is equivalent to 60% of 90?
    a) 0.6 x 90
    b) 90 ÷ 0.6
    c) 3/5
    d) 2/3

3. Convert the improper fraction 17/6 to a mixed number.
    a) $1\frac{7}{6}$
    b) $2\frac{5}{6}$
    c) 6/17
    d) $2\frac{7}{6}$

4. The decimal value of 7/11 is _____?
    a) 1.57
    b) 0.70
    c) 0.6363...
    d) 0.77

5. The decimal value of 5/8 is _____?
    a) 0.625
    b) 0.650
    c) 0.635
    d) 0.580

6. The fractional value of 0.5625 is ____ ?
    a) 7/15
    b) 11/23
    c) 5/8
    d) 9/16

7. The fractional value of 0.3125 is_____?
    a) 5/16
    b) 4/24
    c) 6/19
    d) 9/25

8. What is the value of this expression if a = 10 and b = –4: $\sqrt{b^2 - 2 \times a}$
   a) 6
   b) 7
   c) 8
   d) 9

9. What is the greatest common factor of 48 and 64?
   a) 4
   b) 8
   c) 16
   d) 32

10. Solve for x: $X = \frac{3}{4} \times \frac{7}{8}$
   a) 7/8
   b) 9/8
   c) 10/12
   d) 21/32

11. Find the value of $a^2 + 6b$ when a = 3 and b = 0.5.
   a) 12
   b) 6
   c) 9
   d) 15

12. What is the least common multiple of 8 and 10?
   a) 80
   b) 40
   c) 18
   d) 72

13. What is the sum of 1/3 and 3/8?
   a) 3/24
   b) 4/11
   c) 17/24
   d) 15/16

14. Solve this equation: $-9 \times -9 =$ ___?
   a) 18
   b) 0
   c) 81
   d) –81

15. Which of the following is between 2/3 and 3/4?
    a) 3/5
    b) 4/5
    c) 7/10
    d) 5/8

16. Which digit is in the thousandths place in the number: 1,234.567
    a) 1
    b) 2
    c) 6
    d) 7

17. Which of these numbers is largest?
    a) 5/8
    b) 3/5
    c) 2/3
    d) 0.72

18. Which of these numbers is largest?
    a) −345
    b) 42
    c) −17
    d) 3^4

19. Find 4 numbers between 4.857 and 4.858
    a) 4.8573, 4.85735, 4.85787, 4.8598
    b) 4.857, 4.8573, 4.8578, 4.8579,
    c) 4.8571, 4.8573, 4.8578, 4.8579
    d) 4.8572, 4.8537, 4.8578, 4.8579

20. Which number is between 4 and 5?
    a) 11/3
    b) 21/4
    c) 31/6
    d) 23/5

21. Which number is not between 7 and 9?
    a) 34/5
    b) 29/4
    c) 49/6
    d) 25/3

22. If $\frac{4}{9}x - 3 = 1$, what is the value of x?

    a) 9
    b) 8
    c) 7
    d) −4½

23. What value of q is a solution to this equation: 130 = q(−13)

    a) 10
    b) −10
    c) 1
    d) 10^2

24. Solve this equation: x = −12 ÷ −3

    a) x = −4
    b) x = −15
    c) x = 9
    d) x = 4

25. Solve for r in the equation p = 2r + 3

    a) r = 2p − 3
    b) r = p + 6
    c) r = (p - 3) / 2
    d) r = p − 3/2

26. Solve this equation: x = 8 − (−3)

    a) x = 5
    b) x = −5
    c) x = 11
    d) x = −11

27. Evaluate the expression $7x^2 + 9x -18$ for x =7

    a) 516
    b) 424
    c) 388
    d) 255

28. Evaluate the expression $x^2 + 7x -18$ for x =5

    a) 56
    b) 42
    c) 38
    d) 25

29. Evaluate the expression $7x^2 + 63x$ for $x = 27$
   a) 5603
   b) 4278
   c) 6804
   d) 6525

30. Sam worked 40 hours at d dollars per hour and received a bonus of $50. His total earnings were $530. What was his hourly wage?
   a) $18
   b) $16
   c) $14
   d) $12

31. The variable X is a positive integer. Dividing X by a positive number less than 1 will yield
   a) a number greater than X
   b) a number less than X
   c) a negative number
   d) an irrational number

32. Amanda makes $14 an hour as a bank teller and Oscar makes $24 dollars an hour as an auto mechanic. Both work eight hours a day, five days a week. Which of these equations can be used to calculate how much they make together in a five-day week?
   a) $(14 + 24) \cdot 8 \cdot 5$
   b) $14 \cdot 24 \cdot 8 \cdot 5$
   c) $(14 + 24)(8 + 5)$
   d) $14 + 24 \cdot 8 \cdot 5$

33. Seven added to four-fifths of a number equals fifteen. What is the number?
   a) 10
   b) 15
   c) 20
   d) 25

34. If the sum of two numbers is 360 and their ratio is 7:3, what is the smaller number?
   a) 72
   b) 105
   c) 98
   d) 108

35. Jean buys a textbook, a flash drive, a printer cartridge, and a ream of paper. The flash drive costs three times as much as the ream of paper. The textbook costs three times as much as the flash drive. The printer cartridge costs twice as much as the textbook. The ream of paper costs $10. How much does Jean spend altogether?
    a) $250
    b) $480
    c) $310
    d) $180

36. The area of a triangle equals one-half the base times the height. Which of the following is the correct way to calculate the area of a triangle that has a base of 6 and a height of 9?
    a) $(6 + 9)/2$
    b) $\frac{1}{2}(6 + 9)$
    c) $2(6 \times 9)$
    d) $(6)(9)/2$

37. Calculate the value of this expression: $2 + 6 \bullet 3 \bullet (3 \bullet 4)^2 + 1$
    a) 2,595
    b) 5,185
    c) 3,456
    d) 6,464

38. A rectangle of length and width 3x and x has an area of $3x^2$. Write the area polynomial when the length is increased by 5 units and the width is decreased by 3 units. $(3x+5)(x-3)$
    a) $3x^2 + 14x - 15$
    b) $3x^2 - 4x - 15$
    c) $3x^2 - 5x + 15$
    d) $3x^2 + 4x - 15$

39. A triangle of base and height 4x and 7x has an area of $14x^2$, which is equal $\frac{1}{2}$ times the base times the height. Write the area polynomial when the base is increased by 2 units and the height is increased by 3 units. $\frac{1}{2}(4x+2)(7x+3)$
    a) $14x^2 + 14x + 6$
    b) $14x^2 + 14x + 3$
    c) $14x^2 + 13x + 3$
    d) $14x^2 + 28x + 3$

40. Momentum is defined as the product of mass times velocity. If your 1,250 kg car is travelling at 55 km/hr, what is the value of the momentum?
    a) 68,750 kg m/s
    b) 19,098 kg m/s
    c) 9,549 kg m/s
    d) 145,882 kg m/s

41. In her retirement accounts, Janet has invested $40,000 in stocks and $65,000 in bonds. If she wants to rebalance her accounts so that 70% of her investments are in stocks, how much will she have to move?
    a) $33,500
    b) $35,000
    c) $37,500
    d) $40,000

42. Brian pays 15% of his gross salary in taxes. If he pays $7,800 in taxes, what is his gross salary?
    a) $52,000
    b) $48,000
    c) $49,000
    d) $56,000

43. In a high school French class, 45% of the students are sophomores, and there are 9 sophomores in the class. How many students are there in the class?
    a) 16
    b) 18
    c) 20
    d) 22

44. Marisol's score on a standardized test was ranked in the 78th percentile. If 660 students took the test, approximately how many students scored lower than Marisol?
    a) 582
    b) 515
    c) 612
    d) 486

45. The population of Mariposa County in 2015 was 90% of its population in 2010. The population in 2010 was 145,000. What was the population in 2010?
    a) 160,000
    b) 142,000
    c) 120,500
    d) 130,500

46. Alicia must have a score of 75% to pass a test of 80 questions. What is the greatest number of question she can miss and still pass the test?
    a) 20
    b) 25
    c) 60
    d) 15

47. A cell phone on sale at 30% off costs $210. What was the original price of the phone?
    a) $240
    b) $273
    c) $300
    d) $320

48. In the graduating class at Emerson High School, 52% of the students are girls and 48% are boys. There are 350 students in the class. Among the girls, 98 plan to go to college. How many girls do not plan to go to college?
    a) 84
    b) 48
    c) 66
    d) 72

49. The number of students enrolled at Two Rivers Community College increased from 3,450 in 2010 to 3,864 in 2015. What was the percent increase?
    a) 9%
    b) 17%
    c) 12%
    d) 6%

50. Produce is usually priced to the nearest pound. A scale for weighing produce has numerical values for pounds and ounces. Which of the following weights would you expect to be priced for 15 pounds?
    a) 15 pounds 14 ounces
    b) 15 pounds 10 ounces
    c) 14 pounds 4 ounces
    d) 14 pounds 14 ounces

51. Which number is rounded to the nearest ten-thousandth?
    a) 7,510,000
    b) 7,515,000
    c) 7,514,635.8239
    d) 7,514,635.824

52. Measuring devices determine the precision of our scientific measurements. A graduated cylinder is used that has a maximum of 10 cc's but has ten increments in between each whole number of cc's. Which answer is a correct representation of a volume measurement with this cylinder?
    a) 7 cc's
    b) 7.1 cc's
    c) 7.15 cc's
    d) 7.514 cc's

53. If a man can unload about 50 pounds in a time of 15 minutes, estimate the time and labor force to unload 2.5 tons of 50 pound blocks from a truck working 8 hours per day.
    a) 1 man for 10 days
    b) 2 men for 1 day
    c) 4 men for 1 day
    d) 5 men for 5 days

54. In rush hour, you can usually commute 18 miles to work in 45 minutes. If you believe that you can travel an average of 5 miles per hour faster in the early morning, how much time would you estimate for the early commute to work?
    a) 50 minutes
    b) 40 minutes
    c) 30 minutes
    d) 20 minutes

55. You are taking a test and you are allowed to work a class period of 45 minutes. 20 problems are multiple choice and 30 of the problems are true / false. If they have equal value, how much time would you estimate for each type of problem if you believe you are twice as fast at multiple choice problems?
    a) 90 seconds per m/c; 45 seconds per t/f
    b) 60 seconds per m/c; 30 seconds per t/f
    c) 70 seconds per m/c; 35 seconds per t/f
    d) 80 seconds per m/c; 40 seconds per t/f

56. Your interview is scheduled for 8:00 in the morning and you need to allow 20 minutes for your trip to the interview. You oversleep and leave 10 minutes late. How fast will you travel to get there on time?
    a) half as fast
    b) twice as fast
    c) three times as fast
    d) four times as fast

57. A square meter is a square with sides that are one meter in length. If a meter is 1000 millimeters, how many square millimeters are in a square meter.
    a) 100
    b) 1000
    c) 10,000
    d) 1,000,000

58. In four years, Tom will be twice as old as Serena was three years ago. Tom is three years younger than Serena. How old are Tom and Serena?
    a) Serena is 28, Tom is 25
    b) Serena is 7, Tom is 4
    c) Serena is 18, Tom is 15
    d) Serena is 21, Tom is 18

59. Amy drives her car until the gas gauge is down to 1/8 full. Then she fills the tank by adding 14 gallons. What is the capacity of the gas tank?
    a) 16 gallons
    b) 18 gallons
    c) 20 gallons
    d) 22 gallons

60. Two rectangles are proportional; that is, the ratio of length to width is the same for both rectangles. The smaller rectangle has a length of 8 inches and a width of 3 inches. The large rectangle has a length of 12 inches. What is the width of the larger rectangle?
    a) 4 inches
    b) 4.5 inches
    c) 6 inches
    d) 8.5inches

61. The perimeter of a rectangle is 24 inches, and the ratio of the length to the width is 2:1. What is the area of the rectangle?
    a) 60 square inches
    b) 18 square inches
    c) 32 square inches
    d) 48 square inches

62. The tree near your house casts a shadow of 27 feet. At the same time of day, your house which is 40 feet tall at the peak of the roof casts a shadow of 68 feet. The tree height must be   .
    a) 100 feet tall
    b) 16 feet tall
    c) 45 feet tall
    d) 20 feet tall

63. Five students volunteered to paint a room in the community center. If the painters estimated they would finish the job with 2 ½ man-days, how long should it take the students?
    a) Two days
    b) One day
    c) Half a day
    d) One quarter of a day

64. Your car can maintain 23 miles per gallon on the freeway. If you are travelling to Oklahoma City, which is about 500 miles north, how much gasoline will be required for the trip?
    a) 37 gallons
    b) 53 gallons
    c) 105 gallons
    d) 22 gallons

65. On your trip, you find that it takes you 8.5 hours to get to Oklahoma City which is 500 miles north. How much more time should it take to get to Wichita, Kansas (640 miles total)
    a) 7 hours
    b) 5 hours
    c) 11 hours
    d) 2.5 hours

66. Eight machines can produce 96 parts per minute. How many parts could 12 identical machines produce in 3 minutes?
    a) 144
    b) 288
    c) 256
    d) 432

67. At Pleasantville College, the ratio of female to male students is exactly 5 to 4. Which of the following could be the number of students at the college?
    a) 8,200
    b) 2,955
    c) 3,500
    d) 3,105

68. When you add two numbers, the sum is 480. The ratio of the two numbers is 5:1, what is the smaller number?
    a) 60
    b) 70
    c) 72
    d) 80

69. Four friends plan to share the cost of a retirement gift equally. If one person drops out of the arrangement, the cost per person for the other three would increase by $12. What is the cost of the gift?
    a) $144
    b) $136
    c) $180
    d) $152

70. It took Charles four days to write a history paper. He wrote 5 pages on the first day, 4 pages on the second day, and 8 pages on the third day. If Charles wrote an average of 7 pages per day, how many pages did he write on the fourth day?
    a) 11
    b) 8
    c) 12
    d) 9

71. How much weight must you lose each week if you are determined to lose 63 pounds in 6 months?
    a) 0.4 lbs. per week
    b) 2.4 lbs. per week
    c) 1.4 lbs. per week
    d) 0.64 lbs. per week

72. How much money must you save each week if you are determined to have $375 in the next 7 months?
    a) $12.38 per week
    b) $11.50 per week
    c) $13.75 per week
    d) $7. 75 per week

73. If you think that you can save $450 out of your monthly pay check, how long will it take for you to save $3995 for your car down payment?
    a) 8 months
    b) 10 months
    c) 9 weeks
    d) 9 months

74. You have read that your car is losing value at a rate of $55 per month. You are asking $1790 and a potential buyer has offered you $1450. How many months will it take before you can accept that offer?
    a) 8 months
    b) 6 months
    c) 15 weeks
    d) 4 months

75. The product of two numbers is 6 more than the sum of the two numbers. Which of these equations describes this relationship?
    a) X • Y + 6 = X + Y
    b) X • Y = X + Y+ 6
    c) X + Y = X + Y −6
    d) X • Y = X + Y −6

76. There are 3 more men than women on the board of directors of the Big Box Retail Company. There are 13 members of the board. How many are women?
    a) 3
    b) 4
    c) 5
    d) 6

77. The average of 25, 35, and 120 is 10 more than the average of 40, 45, and which value?
    a) 60
    b) 65
    c) 70
    d) 76

78. What is the smallest positive integer that is evenly divisible by 5 and 7 and leaves a remainder of 4 when divided by 6?
    a) 35
    b) 70
    c) 105
    d) 140

79. The ratio of female to male nurses in a hospital is 9:1. If there are 144 female nurses, how many male nurses are there?
    a) 12
    b) 14
    c) 16
    d) 18

80. Of the patients admitted to an ER over a one-week period, 14 had heart attacks, 15 had workplace injuries, 24 were injured in auto accidents, 12 had respiratory problems, 21 were injured in their homes, and 34 had other problems. What percent of patients had respiratory problems?
    a) 10%
    b) 12%
    c) 15%
    d) 18%

81. Alan commutes 18 miles to work. Bob's commute is 4 miles shorter. Ted's commute is 6 miles shorter than Bob's. Rebecca's commute is shorter than Alan's but longer than Bob's. Which of the following could be the length of Rebecca's commute?
    a) 12 miles
    b) 14 miles
    c) 15 miles
    d) 18 miles

82. At a lunch cart there are 2 orders of diet soda for every 5 orders of regular soda. If the owner of the lunch cart sells 112 sodas a day, how many are diet and how many are regular?
    a) 28 diet, 84 regular
    b) 32 diet, 80 regular
    c) 34 diet, 82 regular
    d) 36 diet, 84 regular

83. The three teams with the best records in the division are the Bulldogs, the Rangers, and the Statesmen. The Bulldogs have won nine games and lost three. The Rangers have won ten games and lost two. The Statesmen have also won ten games and lost two. Each team has one game left before the playoffs. The Bulldogs will be playing the Black Sox, and the Rangers will be playing the Statesmen. The team with the best record will win a spot in the playoffs. Which of the following statements is true?
    a) The Statesmen will definitely be in the playoffs.
    b) The Bulldogs will definitely not be in the playoffs.
    c) The Rangers will definitely not be in the playoffs.
    d) The Statesmen will definitely not be in the playoffs.

84. At Pleasantville College, the ratio of female to male students is exactly 5 to 4. Which of the following could be the number of students at the college?
    a) 8,200
    b) 2,955
    c) 3,500
    d) 3,105

85. Which equation is shown on this graph?

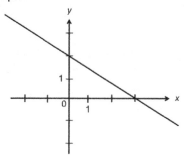

    a) y = 2x + 1
    b) y = −2/3x + 2
    c) y = −3x + 1
    d) y = 3x + 2

86. If the y-intercept of the line on this graph was reduced by 1, what would be the slope of the line?

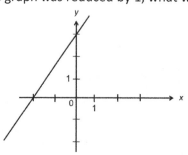

    a) −1
    b) −2
    c) 2
    d) 1

87. Each figure (ß) is valued at $450 . Which of the following is valued closest to $6,500?

  a) ß/2
  b) ß ß ß ß ß ß ß ß ß
  c) ß ß ß ß ß ß ß ß ß ß ß ß ß ß/2
  d) ß ß ß ß ß

88. Kevin has his glucose levels checked monthly. These are the results:

January	February	March	April	May	June	July
98	102	88	86	110	92	90

  In which month was his glucose level equal to the median level for these seven months?

  a) January
  b) March
  c) April
  d) June

89. The average weight of five friends (Al, Bob, Carl, Dave, and Ed) is 180 pounds. Al weighs 202 pounds, Bob weighs 166 pounds, Carl weighs 190 pounds, and Dave weighs 192 pounds. How much does Ed weigh?

  a) 180 pounds
  b) 172 pounds
  c) 186 pounds
  d) 150 pounds

90. What is the mode in this set of numbers: 4, 5, 4, 8, 10, 4, 6, 7

  a) 6
  b) 4
  c) 8
  d) 7

91. Find the median in this series of numbers: 80, 78, 73, 69, 100.

  a) 69
  b) 73
  c) 78
  d) 80

92. Your scholarship requires a 93% average in your Medical Terminology class. Your grades so far are in this class are 88, 90, 95, 92, 87, 89, 90, 95. With two grades left, what average do you need to have for those two grades to maintain your scholarship?

  a) 97
  b) 99
  c) 101
  d) 102

93. The x/y values for your data look like the following table:

X:	3	5	7	9	11	13	15	17
Y:	22	19	16	13	10	7	4	1

The y-intercept is defined as the y value when x = 0. The y-intercept for the data table in this problem is:
a) 8
b) 19.7
c) 25
d) 26.5

94. Which of the following represents the relationship between x and y in this table?

X	Y
0	7
3	13
5	17
7	21
8	23

a) y = x + 7
b) y = 4x + 1
c) y = 2x + 10
d) y = 2x + 7

95. If a patient's weight is recorded each day for a two-week period, a graph of this data would most likely be presented with:
a) y axis with height and x axis with date
b) y axis with weight and x axis with time
c) y axis with dates and x axis with weight
d) y axis with weight and x axis with date

96. The weather channel says that the temperature will be 45 degrees on Monday and increasing 5 degrees each day for the Tuesday through Sunday. With this description, which best describes the dependent and independent variables?
a) The day depends on the temperature
b) Days are the independent variable
c) Temperature is the independent variable
d) There is no correlation between day and temperature

97. A critical care patient has lost 15 pounds during the hospital stay. In terms of the mathematical model of this data, it is labelled as a(n)
a) positive covariation
b) negative covariation
c) independent variable covariation
d) random covariation

98. A rectangle has a length of 8 and a width of 6. What would be the side of a square with the same perimeter?

    a) 5
    b) 6
    c) 7
    d) 8

99. Which of the following can be the lengths of the sides of a triangle?

    a) 1,2,4
    b) 2,4,8
    c) 2,3,4
    d) 4,5,9

100. A square 8 inches on a side is cut into smaller squares 1 inch on a side. How many of the smaller squares can be made?

    a) 8
    b) 16
    c) 24
    d) 64

101. What is the perimeter of this figure?

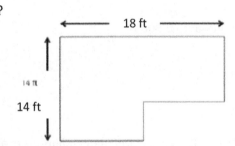

    a) 64 ft.
    b) 72 ft.
    c) 84 ft.
    d) 96 ft.

102. If the radius of the circle in this diagram is 4 inches, what is the perimeter of the square?

    a) 24 inches
    b) 32 inches
    c) 64 inches
    d) 96 inches

103. A rectangle's length is three times its width. The area of the rectangle is 48 square feet. How long are the sides?
    a) length = 12, width = 4
    b) length = 15, width = 5
    c) length = 18, width = 6
    d) length = 24, width = 8

104. Danvers is 8 miles due south of Carson and 6 miles due west of Baines. If a driver could drive in a straight line from Carson to Baines, how long would the trip be?
    a) 8 miles
    b) 10 miles
    c) 12 miles
    d) 14 miles

105. Carmen has a box that is 18 inches long, 12 inches wide, and 14 inches high. What is the volume of the box?
    a) 44 cubic inches
    b) 3,024 cubic inches
    c) 216 cubic inches
    d) 168 cubic inches

106. Which of the following is equal to 0.0065?
    a) 6.5×10^{-2}
    b) 6.5×10^{-3}
    c) 6.5×10^{-4}
    d) 6.5×10^{-5}

107. If one inch is equal to 25.4 millimeters, how many millimeters are in a 20 foot long steel beam?
    a) 6506
    b) 6906
    c) 6609
    d) 6096

108. Medical doses are often measured in cubic centimeters or cc's. A rectangular volume that has a volume of 100 cc's and a square base with 4 inches on each side must must be how tall?
    a) 9.7 millimeters
    b) 6.5 centimeters
    c) 103 centimeters
    d) 10.3 millimeters

109. Small motorcycles often have a displacement of 100 cc's or less. This represents ___ cubic inches?
    a) 61 cubic inches
    b) 15.5 cubic inches
    c) 6.1 cubic inches
    d) 39.4 cubic inches

110. A medical dose is listed as 25 milligrams for each capsule. If there are thirty capsules in the bottle. How many kilograms of the drug are in the bottle?
    a) 0.00075 kg
    b) 750 g
    c) 250 g
    d) 0.00050 kg

Mathematics Practice Test – Answer Key

<u>1 – C. 7/3</u>
Rationale: An improper fraction is a fraction whose numerator is greater than its denominator. To change a mixed number to an improper fraction, multiply the whole number (2) times the denominator (3) and add the result to the numerator. Answer C is the correct choice.

<u>2 – A. 0.6 x 90</u>
Rationale: To find 60% of 90, first convert 60% to a decimal by moving the decimal point two places to the left. Then multiply this decimal, 0.6, times 90. Answer A is the correct choice.

<u>3 – B. 2 5/6</u>
Rationale: To convert an improper fraction to a mixed number, divide the numerator by the denominator. In this case, you get 2 with a remainder of 5. 2 becomes the whole number and the remainder is the numerator. Answer B is the correct choice.

<u>4 – C. 0.6363…</u>
Rationale – The ratio 7/11 implies division, so the decimal value can be determined by the long division problem of 7 divided by11. The long division results in the repeating decimal 0.6363… There may be a simpler method to find this decimal. The ratio 7/11 is the product of 7 times 1/11. The ratio 1/11 is the repeating decimal 0.0909… so multiplying that decimal by 7 is 0.6363… provides the same answer. If it seems like the same amount of effort, remember that every fraction with 11 in the denominator can be determined in the same way. Answer C is the correct choice.

<u>5 – A. 0.625</u>
Rationale – The ratio implies division, so 5/8 can be determined by the long division problem of 5 divided by 8. The long division results in the decimal 0.625. There is a simpler method to find this decimal. The ratio 5/8 is the product of 5 times 1/8. The ratio 1/8 is the decimal 0.125 so multiplying that decimal by 5 is 0.625, which is the same answer. If it seems like the same amount of effort, remember that every fraction with 8 in the denominator can be determined in the same way. Answer A is the correct choice.

<u>6 – D. 9/16</u>
Rationale – The numerator in the correct ratio will be equal to the given decimal times the correct denominator. It is simply a result of cross multiplying. But first, these problems can be greatly simplified if we eliminate incorrect answers.

For example, answers A and B can both be eliminated because they are both less than 0.5 or ½. If you can't see that, then multiply .5 times 15 and .5 times 23. In answer A, .5 times 15 is 7.5 so 7/15 is less than the fractional value of 0.5625. In B, .5 times 23 is 11.5 so 11/23 is less than the fractional value of 0.5625.

Now, evaluating fractional answers this way, you may look at answer C and realize that since 0.6 times 8 equals 4.8. Since 4.8 is less than the numerator and 0.6 is larger than the given decimal value, C can be eliminated. Answer D is the correct choice.

<u>7 – A. 5/16</u>
Rationale – The numerator in the correct ratio will be equal to the given decimal times the correct denominator. It is simply a result of cross multiplying. But first, the problem can be simplified if we eliminate impossible answers.

For example, answer B can be eliminated because it simplifies to 1/6 which is much less than 0.3125. If you can't see that, then divide 1 by 6 which becomes 0.167.

For answer D, the ratio 9/25 is a simplified form of 36/100 or 0.36. 0.36 is greater than 0.3125, so answer D can be eliminated.

Now, evaluating fractional answers this way, you may eliminate answer C for a very simple reason. 19 times 0.3125 will always leave a value of 5 in the ten-thousandths place because 19 times 5 equals 95. That means the product can never be the whole number 6, so answer C can be eliminated.

The correct answer is D because you have logically eliminated all the other possible choices.

8 – A. 6
Rationale: If a = 10, then 2a = 20. Now compute the value of b2

$b^2 = (b) \bullet (b)$

$b^2 = (-4) \bullet (-4)$

$b^2 = 16$

So now you have: 16 + 20   *or*   36

The square root of 36 is 6. Answer A is the correct choice

9 – C. 16
Rationale: The greatest common factor of two numbers is the largest number that can be divided evenly into both numbers. The simplest way to answer this question is to start with the largest answer (32) and see if it can be divided evenly into 48 and 64. It can't. Now try the next largest answer (16), and you see that it can be divided evenly into 48 and 64. 16 is the correct answer. The other answers are also factors but the largest of them is 16. Answer C is the correct choice

10 – D. 21/32
Rationale: To multiply fractions, multiply the numerators and the denominators. In this case, multiply 3 times 7 and 4 times 8. The answer is 21/32. Answer D is the correct choice.

11 – A. 12
Rationale: Replace the letters with the numbers they represent and then perform the necessary operations.

$3^2 + 6(0.5)$

9 + 3 = 12

Answer A is the correct choice.

12 – B. 40
Rationale: The least common multiple is used when finding the lowest common denominator. The least common multiple is the lowest number that can be divided evenly by both of the other numbers.

Here is a simple method to find the least common multiple of 8 and 10. Write 8 on the left side of your paper. Then add 8 and write the result. Then add another 8 to that number and write the result. Keep going until you have a list that looks something like this:
8 16 24 32 40…

This is a partial list of multiples of 8. (If you remember your multiplication tables, these numbers are the column or row that go with 8.)

Now do the same thing with 10.

10 20 30 40…
This is the partial list of multiples of 10.

Eventually, the numbers will be found in both rows. That smallest common number is the least common multiple. There will always be more multiples that are common to both rows, but the smallest number is the least common multiple.

Answer B is the correct choice

13 – C. 17/24
Rationale: To add 1/3 and 3/8, you must find a common denominator. The simplest way to do this is to multiply the denominators: 3 x 8 = 24. So 24 is a common denominator. (This method will not always give you the lowest common denominator, but in this case it does.)

Once you have found a common denominator, you need to convert both fractions in the problem to equivalent fractions that have that same denominator. To do this, multiply each fraction by an equivalent of 1.

1/3 ● 8/8 = (8●1) / (8●3) or 8/24

3/8 ● 3/3 = (3●3) / (8●3) or 9/24.
8/24 + 9/24 = 17/24

Adding 8/24 and 9/24 is the solution to the problem. Answer C is the correct choice.

14 – C. 81
Rationale: When two numbers with the same sign (both positive or both negative) are multiplied, the answer is a positive number. When two numbers with different signs (one positive and the other negative) are multiplied, the answer is negative. Answer C is the correct choice.

15 – C. 7/10
Rationale: The simplest way to solve this problem is to convert the fractions to decimals. You do this by dividing the numerators by the denominators.

2/3 = 0.67 and 3/4 = 0.75, so the correct answer is a decimal that falls between these two numbers.

3/5 = 0.6 (too small) 4/5 = 0.8 (too large)
7/10 = 0.7 (correct choice between 0.67 and 0.75 5/8 = 0.625 (too small)

Answer C is the correct choice

16 – D. 7
Rationale: In this number:
1 is in the thousands place. 2 is in the hundreds place. 3 is in the tens place.
 4 is in the ones place 5 is in the tenths place.

6 is in the hundredths place. 7 is in the thousandths place.

Answer D is the correct choice.

17 – D. 0.72
Rationale: The simplest way to answer this question is to convert the fractions to decimals. To convert a fraction to a decimal, divide the numerator (the top number) by the denominator (the bottom number).
5/8 = 0.625
3/5 = 0.6
2/3 = 0.67

So the largest number is 0.72. Answer D is the correct choice.

18 – D. 3^4
Rationale: All positive numbers are larger than the negative numbers, so the possible answers are 42 or 3^4. 3^4 equals 81 (3 • 3 • 3 • 3). Answer D is the correct choice.

19 – C. 4.8571, 4.8573, 4.8578, 4.8579
Rationale: The numbers 4.857 and 4.858 have an unlimited set of numbers between them and the simplest method is to start with another number after the last digit of 4.857. Therefore 4.8571 and 4.8572 are both greater than 4.857 and less than 4.858. Choices A, B, and D, include numbers that are equal to or greater than the larger of the two or less than the two numbers. Only C has all numbers between. Answer C is the correct choice

20 – D. 23/5
Rationale: The numbers 4 and 5 can be multiplied by the denominators in the answer set to see which answers are correct. Only D is correct because 20/5 and 25/5 are the numbers that are less than and greater than the answer 23/5. Answer D is the correct choice.

21 – A. 34/5
Rationale: The numbers 7 and 9 can be multiplied by the denominators in the answer set to see which answers are correct. A is correct because 34/5 is less than 35/5 and 45/5, so it can't be in between. Answer A is the correct choice.

22 – A. 9
Rationale: Begin by subtracting –3 from both sides of the equation. (This is the same as adding +3). Then:

$$\frac{4}{9}x = 4$$

Now to isolate X on one side of the equation, divide both sides by 4/9. (To divide by a fraction, invert the fraction and multiply).

$$\frac{9}{4} * \frac{4}{9}X = \frac{4}{1} * \frac{9}{4}$$

You are left with $x = \frac{36}{4} = 9$. Answer A is the correct choice.

23 – B. –10
Rationale: To find the value of q, divide both sides of the equation by –13. When a positive number is divided by a negative number, the answer is negative. Answer B is the correct choice.

24 – D. x = 4

Rationale: When you multiply or divide numbers that have the same sign (both positive or both negative), the answer will be positive. When you multiply or divide numbers that have different signs (one positive and the other negative), the answer will be negative. In this case, both numbers have the same sign. Divide as you normally would and remember that the answer will be a positive number. Answer D is the correct choice.

25 – C. r = (p - 3) / 2

Rationale: Begin by subtracting 3 from both sides of the equation. You get:

p – 3 = 2r

Now to isolate r on one side of the equation, divide both sides of the equation by 2. You get:
r = (p-3) / 2

Answer C is the correct choice

26 – C. x = 11

Rationale: Subtracting a negative number is the same as adding a positive number. So 8 – (–3) is the same as 8 + 3 or 11. Answer C is the correct choice.

27 – C. 388

Rationale – The value can be expanded as 7 x 49 added to 9 x 7 with 18 subtracted from the total. That becomes 343 + 63 -18 with the answer equal to 388. Answer C is the correct choice.

28 – B. 42

Rationale – The value can be expanded as 25 added to 5 x 7 with 18 subtracted from the total. That becomes 25 + 35 -18 with the answer equal to 42. There is another simple way to evaluate this expression. The expression can be rewritten as the product of two expressions (x+9)(x-2). If we substitute 5 for x then this product becomes 14 x 3 which is also 42. Answer B is the correct choice.

29 – C. 6804

Rationale – The simplest way to evaluate this expression is to rewrite it as the product of two expressions. Factoring common factors out the given expression becomes 7x(x + 9). "7x" becomes 189 and x+9 becomes 36. The product of 189 and 36 becomes 6804. In the interest of eliminating incorrect answers, the product of the values in the "ones" column is 6x9 which is 54. The correct answer must end in 4 so the correct answer must be C. Answer C is the correct choice.

30 – D. $12

Rationale: Use the information given to write an equation: 530 = 40d + 50

When you subtract 50 from both sides of the equation, you get: 480 = 40d

Divide both sides of the equation by 40.

12 = d, Sam's hourly wage Answer D is the correct choice.

<u>31 – A. a number greater than X</u>
Rationale: When a positive number is divided by a positive number less than 1, the quotient will always be larger than the number being divided. For example, 5 ÷ 0.5 = 10. If we solve this as a fraction, 5÷ (1/2) is the same as 5 x (2/1) or 10 since dividing by a fraction is the same as multiplying by the reciprocal. Answer A is the correct choice.

<u>32 – A. (14 + 24) • 8 • 5</u>
Rationale: In the correct answer, (14 + 24) • 8 • 5, the hourly wages of Amanda and Oscar are first combined, and the total amount is multiplied by 8 hours in a day and five days in a week. One of the other choices, 14 + 24 • 8 • 5, looks similar to this, but it is incorrect because the hourly wages must be combined before they can be multiplied by 8 and 5. Answer A is the correct choice

<u>33 – A. 10</u>
 Rationale: Use the facts you are given to write an equation:

7 + 4/5n = 15

First subtract 7 from both side of the equation. You get:

4/5n = 8

Now divide both sides of the equation by 4/5. To divide by a fraction, invert the fraction (4/5 becomes 5/4) and multiply:

(5/4)4/5n = 8•5/4

n = 40/4 or 10. Answer A is the correct choice

<u>34 – D. 108</u>
Rationale: The ratio of the two numbers is 7:3. This means that the larger number is 7/10 of 360 and the smaller number is 3/10 of 360.

The larger number is 7 • 360/10 or 7 • 36 or 252
The smaller number is 3 • 360/10 or 3 • 36 or 108 Answer D is the correct choice.

<u>35 – C. $310</u>
Rationale: The costs of all these items can be expressed in terms of the cost of the ream of paper. Use x to represent the cost of a ream of paper. The flash drive costs three times as much as the ream of paper, so it costs 3x. The textbook costs three times as much as the flash drive, so it costs 9x. The printer cartridge costs twice as much as the textbook, so it costs 18x. So now we have:
x + 3x + 9x + 18x = 31x

The ream of paper costs $10, so 31x, the total cost, is $310. Answer C is the correct choice

<u>36 – D.</u> $\frac{(6)(9)}{2}$
Rationale: The area of a triangle is one-half the product of the base and the height. Choices A and B are incorrect because they add the base and the height instead of multiplying them. Choice C is incorrect because it multiplies the product of the base and the height by 2 instead of dividing it by 2. Answer D is the correct choice.

<u>37 – A. 2,595</u>

Rationale: The steps in evaluating a mathematical expression must be carried out in a certain order, called the order of operations. These are the steps in order:

Parentheses: The first step is to do any operations in parentheses.

Exponents: Then do any steps that involve exponents Multiply and Divide: Multiply and divide from left to right Add and Subtract: Add and subtract from left to right

One way to remember this order is to use this sentence:
Please Excuse My Dear Aunt Sally.
To evaluate the expression in this question, follow these steps: Multiply the numbers in Parentheses:
 $3 \cdot 4 = 12$
Apply the Exponent 2 to the number in parentheses: $12^2 = 144$
Multiply: $6 \cdot 3 \cdot 144 = 2,592$
Add: $2 + 2,592 + 1 = 2,595$

Answer A is the correct choice.

<u>38 – B. $3x^2$ - 4x - 15</u>

Rationale – The words in the problem tell us that the new expression for the length is 3x+5 and the new width is represented by the expression x-3. The area is represented by the product of (3x+5) (x-3). Multiplying the two binomials together with FOIL means that the first term is the product of x and 3x or $3x^2$. All of the multiple choices have the correct first term. However, the last term is the product of 5 and -3, or -15, which means that answer C is an incorrect answer.

Since the middle term is the difference of 5x and -9x, which is -4x, answer B is the only correct answer. If you choose to use the box method to solve these products, you will see the same results and the same factors. Answer B is the correct choice.

<u>39 – C. $14x^2$ +13x + 3</u>

Rationale – The words in the problem tell us that the new expression for the base is 4x+2 and the new height is represented by the expression 7x+3. The area is represented by the product of 1/2(4x+2) (7x+3). Multiplying the two binomials together with FOIL means that the first term is the product of 4x and 7x and ½ or $14x^2$.

However, the last term is the product of 2 and 3 and 1/2, or 3, which means that answer A is an incorrect answer.

The middle term is ½ the sum of 14x and 12x which is 26/2 x or 13x. Therefore answer C is the only correct answer.

<u>40 – B. 19,098 kg m/s</u>

Rationale – Momentum is defined as the product of mass times velocity. The conversion of 55 km/hr to meters per second means multiplying by one thousand and dividing by 3600. (seconds per hour). That value,15.28, must be multiplied by the 1,250 kg mass. That answer is 19,098 kg m/s. Answer B is the correct choice.

41 – A. $33,500
Rationale: Janet has a total of $105,000 in her accounts. 70% of that amount, her goal for her stock investments, is $73,500. To reach that goal, she would have to move
$33,500 from bonds to stocks. Answer A is the correct choice.

42 – A. $52,000
Rationale: Convert 15% to a decimal by moving the decimal point two places to the left: 15% = 0.15. Using x to represent Brian's gross salary, you can write this equation:

0.15 x = $7,800

To solve for x, divide both sides of the equation by 0.15. $7,800 divided by 0.15 is
$52,000. Answer A is the correct choice.

43 – C. 20
Rationale: To solve this problem, first convert 45% to a decimal by moving the decimal point two place to the left: 45% = .45. Use x to represent the total number of students in the class. Then: .45x = 9
Solve for x by dividing both sides of the equation by 0.45.
9 divided by .45 is 20. Answer C is the correct choice.

44 – B. 515
Rationale: Marisol scored higher than 78% of the students who took the test. Convert 78% to a decimal by moving the decimal point two places to the left: 78% = .78. Now multiply .78 times the number of students who took the test:

.78 x 660 = 514.8 or 515 students (whole number answers) Answer B is the correct choice.

45 – D. 130,500
Rationale: The population of Mariposa County in 2015 was 90% of its population in 2010. Convert 90% to a decimal by moving the decimal point two places to the left: 90%
= .90. Now multiply .90 times 145,000, the population in 2010.

.90 • 145,000 = 130,500

Answer D is the correct choice.

46 – A. 20
Rationale: Alicia must have a score of 75% on a test with 80 questions. To find how many questions she must answer correctly, first convert 75% to a decimal by moving the decimal point two places the left: 75% = .75.
Now multiply .75 times 80:

.75 • 80 = 60.

Alicia must answer 60 questions correctly, but the question asks how many questions can she miss. If she must answer 60 correctly, then she can miss 20. Answer A is the correct choice.

47 – C. $300
Rationale: If the phone was on sale at 30% off, the sale price was 70% of the original price.
So $210 = 70% of x
where x is the original price of the phone. When you convert 70% to a decimal, you get:

$210 = .70 • x

To isolate x on one side of the equation, divide both sides of the equation by .70. You find that x = $300. Answer C is the correct choice

48 – A. 84
Rationale: First, find the number of girls in the class. Convert 52% to a decimal by moving the decimal point two places to the left:

52% = .52

Then multiply .52 times the number of students in the class:

.52 • 350 = 182

182 – 98 = 84

Of the 182 girls, 98 plan to go to college, so a total of 84 do not plan to go to college. Answer A is the correct choice

49 – C. 12%
Rationale: To find the percent increase, you first need to know the amount of the increase. Enrollment went from 3,450 in 2010 to 3,864 in 2015. This is an increase of
414. Now, to find the percent of the increase, divide the amount of the increase by the original amount:

414 ÷ 3,450 = 0.12

To convert a decimal to a percent, move the decimal point two places to the right:

0.12 = 12%

When a question asks for the percent increase or decrease, divide the amount of the increase or decrease by the original value. Answer C is the correct choice.

50 – D. 14 pounds 14 ounces
Rationale: When rounding measurements to the whole number value, the measurement is usually rounded up to the next larger whole number if that measurement is halfway or closer to the next higher value. In this case, since there 16 ounces in a pound, D is the correct answer.

51 – C. 7,514,635.8239
Rationale: When rounding a number to a given place value, the next lower place value is used to determine if the number is rounded up or down. The rounded value has its last significant digit in that place. Answer C has a number 9 in the ten thousandths place. Notice the difference between ten-thousands and ten-thousandths. Answer A is rounded to the ten-thousands place!

52 – C. 7.15 cc's
Rationale: When rounding a measurement, the value includes a precision of plus or minus half of the smallest increment measured. The lines on the cylinder would have the values of 7.00, 7.10, 7.20, or each tenth of a cc. The actual value of the meniscus that reads between tenths would be 7.15 cc. Answer C has a number with the correct precision.

<u>53 – C. 4 men for 1 day</u>

A. 1 man for 10 days
B. 2 men for 1 day
C. _____
D. 5 men for 5 days

Rationale: When estimating, it is helpful to round before estimating. The summary of this problems solution includes a rate of 200 pounds per hour (15 minute each). Two and one-half tons is 5000 pounds. 5000 pounds divided by 200 pounds per hour means 25 hours of labor is required. Answer C is the best estimate of 25 hours of labor (32).
Answer A is 800 hours, B is 16 hours, and D is 200 hours.

<u>54– B. 40 minutes</u>
Rationale: When estimating this answer, the basic formula of distance equal to rate multiplied by time applies. So the time required for the trip is the distance divided by the rate. 18 miles divide by ¾ (45 minutes is ¾ of an hour), is 24 miles per hour. The new rate would be 29 miles per hour (increase of 5). 18 divided by 29 is about 60% of an hour or close to 40 minutes. 30 minutes is a close answer, but that is only possible if the rate is 36 miles per hour! Estimating may require that you eliminate answers that are close to the correct answer. Answer B is the correct choice

<u>55 – C. 70 seconds per m/c; 35 seconds per t/f</u>
Rationale: An estimate often means that you will need to check possible answers to see if they are correct. In this example, the basic assumption is that the time for m/c problems will be twice the value for the t/f. Trying one minute for m/c and one half minute for t/f comes out to 35 minutes. So answer B is not correct. The next closest one is answer C which comes out to 1400 seconds and 1050 seconds for the total 2450 seconds. That is close to the allowable 2700 seconds (45 minutes). If you try answer D, the total comes out to 1600 plus 1200 or a total of 2800 seconds. That's more than the allowable total of 2700. Answer C is the correct choice.

<u>56 – B. twice as fast</u>
Rationale: When estimating this answer, the formula of distance equal to rate multiplied by time applies. So the speed required for the trip is the distance divided by the time. In this example 10 minutes late means half the amount of time. Dividing by one-half means that the rate must be doubled. Answer B is the correct choice.

<u>57 – D. 1,000,000</u>
Rationale: The number of square units in this square meter is determined by 1000 rows of 1000 squares of 1 millimeter square units each. 1000 multiplied by 1000 is 1,000,000 units. Answer D is the correct choice.

<u>58 – B. Serena is 7, Tom is 4</u>
Rationale: Use S to represent Serena's age. Tom is 3 years younger than Serena, so his age is S–3. In 4 years, Tom will be twice as old as Serena was 3 years ago. So you can write this equation:

Tom + 4 = 2(Serena – 3) Now substitute S for Serena and S–3 for Tom.
(S–3) + 4 = 2(S–3)

Simplify the equation.

S + 1 = 2S – 6

Subtract S from both sides of the equation:

1 = S − 6

Add 6 to both sides of the equation:

7 = S. Serena's age

4 = S-3, Tom's age
Answer B is the correct choice.

59 – A. 16 gallons
Rationale: Amy drives her car until the gas tank is 1/8 full. This means that it is 7/8 empty. She fills it by adding 14 gallons. In other words, 14 gallons is 7/8 of the tank's capacity. Draw a simple diagram to represent the gas tank.

You can see that each eighth of the tank is 2 gallons. So the capacity of the tank is 2 x 8 or 16. Answer A is the correct choice.

60 – B. 4.5 inches
Rationale: The length of the larger rectangle is 12 inches and the length of the smaller rectangle is 8 inches. So the length of the larger rectangle is 1.5 times the length of the smaller rectangle. Since the rectangles are proportional, the width of the larger rectangle must be 1.5 times the width of the smaller rectangle.

1.5 • 3 inches = 4.5 inches Answer B is the correct choice.

61 – C. 32 square inches
Rationale: The perimeter of the rectangle is 24 inches. This means that the length plus the width must equal half of 24, or 12 inches. The ratio of length to width is 2:1, so the length is 2/3 of 12 and the width is 1/3 of 12. The length is 8 inches and the width is 4 inches. The area (length times width) is 32 square inches. Answer C is the correct choice.

62 – B. 16 feet tall
Rationale: The ratio of the shadow length and the actual height is a constant determined by the sun. The ratios that apply are tree height / 27 equals 40 / 68. We solve these ratios by multiplying 27 times 40 divided by 67. The correct answer is B.

63 – C. Half a day
Rationale: The rate for the room is 2.5 man-days per room. The students can apply 5 man-days in one day. One half of a day (answer C) is the required amount of time.

64– D. 22 gallons
Rationale: The rate is defined by 23 miles per gallon. The distance divided by the rate is about 21.7 gallons. Answer D is the correct choice.

65 – D. 2.5 hours
Rationale: The rate is defined by 500 miles per 8.5 hours. That rate means that 140 more miles will require about 2.38 hours (cross multiply 140 • 8.5 and divide by 500). Answer D is the correct choice.

<u>66 – D. 432</u>
Rationale: Each machine can produce 12 parts per minute (96 ÷ 8). Multiply 12 times 12 (12 machines) times 3 (minutes). Answer D is the correct choice.

<u>67 – D. 3,105</u>
Rationale: The ratio of female to male students is exactly 5 to 4, so 5/9 of the students are female and 4/9 of the students are male. This means that the total number of students must be evenly divisible by 9, and 3,105 is the only answer that fits this requirement. Answer D is the correct choice.

<u>68 – D. 80</u>
Rationale: If we call the smaller number x, then the larger number is 5x. The sum of the two numbers is 480, so:
x + 5x = 480 6x = 480
x = 80

Answer D is the correct choice.

<u>69 – A. $144</u>
Rationale: When one person dropped out of the arrangement, the cost for the other three went up by $12 per person, for a total of $36. This means that each person's share was originally $36. There were four people in the original arrangement, so the cost of the gift was 4 x $36 or $144.
Let 4x equal the original cost of the gift. If the number of shares decreases to 3 then the total cost is 3(x+12). Then those expressions must be equal, so :

4x = 3(x+12)
4x = 3x +36

Subtracting 3x from both sides:
X = 36

Then the original price of the gift is 4 time 36 of $144. Answer A is the correct choice.

<u>70 – A. 11</u>
Rationale: If Charles wrote an average of 7 pages per day for four days, he wrote a total of 28 pages. He wrote a total of 17 pages on the first three days, so he must have written 11 pages on the fourth day. Answer A is the correct choice.

<u>71 – B. 2.4 lbs. per week</u>
Rationale – Six months is half of a year and a year is 52 weeks. The rate will be determined by dividing the total amount by 26 weeks. The rate is therefore 63/26 or about 2.4 pounds per week. Answer B is the correct choice.

<u>72 – A. $12.38 per week</u>
Rationale – Seven months out of a year is (52 • 7) / 12 weeks. The rate will be determined by dividing the total amount by 30.3 weeks. The rate is therefore $375/ 30.3 weeks or about $12.38 per week. Answer A is the correct choice.

73 – D. 9 months
Rationale – $3995 divided by $450 per month will provide an answer in months. Numerically the value of that ratio is about 8.88. Since that partial month can't be used, it means that a full nine months will be required to get the full amount. Answer D is the correct choice.

74 – B. 6 months
Rationale – The difference between the offer and your asking price is $1790 – $1450 or $340. Dividing that value by the monthly decrease equals 340/55 or about 6.18 months. Rounding that value to 6 months, you can now evaluate the acceptability of the reduced offer. Since the partial month can be used as part of your decision process, rounding down to the six months is somewhat a judgment for the seller on the value of the money compared to the value of the car. Answer B is the correct choice.

75 – B. X • Y = X + Y+ 6
Rationale: The product of the two numbers is X times Y or X • Y. Therefore, X • Y equals the sum of the two numbers (X + Y) plus 6. Answer B is the correct choice.

76 – C. 5
Rationale: Use x to represent the number of women on the board. Then the number of men is x + 3. So:
x + (x + 3) = 2x +3 = 13

To isolate 2x on one side of the equation, subtract 3 from both sides.

2x = 10
x = 5
Answer B is the correct choice.

77 – B. 65
Rationale: The average of 25, 35, and 120 is 60. 60 is 10 more than the average of the second set of numbers, so the average of the second set of numbers must be 50. The three numbers in the second set of numbers must add up to 150. Subtract 40 and 45 from 150 to get the answer of 65. Answer B is the correct choice.

78 – B. 70
Rationale: Try each of the answers to see if it fits the requirements in the question. The numbers divisible by both 5 and 7 are 35, 70, 105, 140, 175...
The multiples of 6 are 6, 12, 18, 24, 30, 36, 42, 48, 54, 60, 66, 72, 78... Since 70 – 66 = 4; the correct number is 70. Answer B is the correct choice

79 – C. 16
Rationale: There are 9 times as many female nurses as male nurses. To find the number of male nurses, divide the number of female nurses by 9: 144 ÷ 9 = 16. Answer C is the correct choice

80 – A. 10%
Rationale: First find the total number of patients admitted to the ER by adding the number admitted for all the reasons given in the question. A total of 120 patients were admitted. To find the percent that were admitted for respiratory problems, divide the number admitted for respiratory problems by the total number admitted:

12 ÷ 120 = .10

Convert this decimal to percent by moving the decimal point two places to the right: .10

= 10%. When you are asked what percent of a total is a certain part, divide the part by the whole. Answer A is the correct choice

81 – C. 15 miles
Rationale: Rebecca's commute is shorter than Alan's but longer than Bob's. Alan's commute is 18 miles and Bob's is 14 miles, so Rebecca's must be longer than 14 but shorter than 18. Neither 14 nor 18 is correct since the distances cannot be equal to either of the examples. So 15 is the only correct answer. Answer C is the correct choice

82 – B. 32 diet, 80 regular
Rationale: If the owner sells 2 diet sodas for every 5 regular sodas, then 2/7 of the sodas sold are diet and 5/7 are regular. Multiply these fractions times the total number of sodas sold:
2/7 x 112 = 32
5/7 x 112 = 80

Remember: when multiplying a fraction times a whole number, it is usually simpler to divide by the denominator first and then multiply by the numerator. Answer B is the correct choice

83 – B. The Bulldogs will definitely not be in the playoffs.
Rationale: The Rangers are playing the Statesmen in the final game, so one of these teams will finish with a record of eleven wins and two losses. Even if the Bulldogs win their game, their final record will be ten wins and three losses. So the Bulldogs will not be in the playoffs. Answer B is the correct choice

84 – D. 3,105
Rationale: The ratio of female to male students is exactly 5 to 4, so 5/9 of the students are female and 4/9 of the students are male. This means that the total number of students must be evenly divisible by 9, and 3,105 is the only answer that fits this requirement. Answer D is the correct choice

85 – B. y = –2/3x + 2
Rationale: The formula for a linear equation is y = mx +b. m is the slope of the line to be graphed and b is the y-intercept, the point where the line meets the y axis.

The slope of the line in this graph is negative because it is moving downward from left to right. So the number before the x will be negative. Answers A and D cannot be correct answers. The slope of the line is expressed as rise/run. The slope of this line is –2/3 run because it crosses the y axis at 2 and the x axis at 3. The y-intercept, the point where the line crosses the y axis, is 2. The correct equation must be y = –2/3x + 2. Answer B is the correct choice

86. D - 1
Rationale: If the y intercept of the line on this graph was reduced by 1, the line would cross the y axis at 2. The slope of a line is defined as rise/run. You might also describe the run slope of a line as "the change in y over the change in x". If the y intercept was changed to 2, the slope of the line would be 2/2 or 1. The slope of this line is positive because it is moving upward from left to right. Answer D is the correct choice

87 – C. ß ß ß ß ß ß ß ß ß ß ß ß ß ß ß/2
Rationale: If the figures are valued at $450, then dividing $6500 by $450 is 14.44 . C has 14.5 figures which is closest to $6500. Answer C is the correct choice.

<u>88 – D. June</u>
Rationale: To find the median in a series of numbers, arrange the numbers in order from smallest to largest. The number in the center, 92 in this case, is the median. Answer D is the correct choice

<u>89 – D. 150 pounds</u>
Rationale: The average weight of the five friends is 180 pounds, so the total weight of all five is 5 times 180 or 900 pounds. Add the weights of Al, Bob, Carl, and Dave. Together they weigh 750 pounds. Subtract 750 from 900 to find Ed's weight of 150 pounds.
Answer D is the correct choice

<u>90 – B. 4</u>
Rationale: The mode is the number that appears "most often" in a set of numbers. Since 4 appears three times, it is the "Mode". Answer B is the correct choice

<u>91 – C. 78</u>
Rationale: To find the median in a series of numbers, arrange the numbers in order from smallest to largest:
69, 73, 78, 80, 100

The number in the center is the median. Answer C is the correct choice NOTE: If there is an even number of values in the series, for example:
34, 46, 52, 54, 67, 81

then the median will be the average of the two numbers in the center. In this example, the median will be 53, the average of 52 and 54. Remember: the median is not the same as the average. Answer C is the correct choice.

<u>92 – D. 102</u>
Rationale: To find the mean or average, total all the values and divide by the number of values in the sample. In this example there will be 10 grades with an average of 93 points for a total of 930 points. Subtracting the total of points already scored, there are 204 points which are needed to maintain the average. 204 points divided by 2 grades is 102 points per grade. Answer D is the correct choice.

<u>93 – D. 26.5</u>
Rationale: To find the y-intercept, the patterns in the table must be extended until the x value of the table is equal to 0. Extending the data table to the left means the next two data entries will be 1 and -1. The next two y entries will be 25 and 28. Since 0 is midway between 1 and -1, the y-intercept is midway between 25 and 28. The correct value is 26.5. Answer D is the correct choice.

<u>94 – D. y = 2x + 7</u>
Rationale: The simplest way to answer this question is to see which of the equations would work for all the values of x and y in the table.

Choices A and D would work when x = 0 and y = 7, but A would not work for any other values of x and y. Choice B would work when x = 3 and y = 13, but it would not work for any other values of x and y. Choice C would not work for any of the values of x and y.

Only choice D would be correct for each ordered pair in the table

Rationale: The data recorded on a "daily" basis implies that the independent data is the time or date of the test. Independent data is normally recorded on the "x-axis".
Answers A and D are the two possible correct choices. Since the "weight" is the selected data to be recorded, Answer D is the correct choice.

96 – B. Days are the independent variable
Rationale: The weather data reported on a "daily" basis implies that the temperature data is independent. Since time or date is normally the independent data. Answer B is the correct choice.

97 – B. negative covariation
Rationale: The patient's weight data in this problem is a decreasing value in relation to time. Decreasing as a function of increasing x values is the definition of negative covariation. Answer B is the correct choice.

98 – C. 7
 Rationale: The perimeter of the rectangle is 28: 8 + 8 + 6 + 6. If the perimeter of a square is 28, each side is 7. Answer C is the correct choice.

99 – C. 2,3,4
Rationale: The two shorter sides of a triangle must always add up to a value greater than the longest side. Answer C is the correct choice.

100 – D. 64
Rationale: A diagram of the larger square, could be made with 8 rows of 8 smaller squares, so you can make a total of 64 squares. Answer D is the correct choice.

101 – A. 64 ft.
Rationale: We know the dimensions of the left side and the top side of this figure, but how can we find the dimensions of the other sides? Look at the two horizontal lines on the bottom of the figure. We know that together they are as long as the top side of the figure, so together they must total 18 ft. Similarly, the two vertical lines on the right side of the figure, must be as long as the left side of the figure and together they must be 14 ft. So now we know that the perimeter of the figure is 14 + 18 + 14 + 18 or 32 +32 =64. Answer A is the correct choice.

102 – B. 32 inches
Rationale: The radius of a circle is one-half the diameter, so the diameter of this circle is 8 inches. The diameter is a line passing through the center of a circle and joining two points on its circumference. If you study this figure, you can see that the diameter of the circle is the same as the length of each side of the square. The diameter is 8 inches, so the perimeter of the square is 32 inches (8+ 8 + 8 + 8). Answer B is the correct choice.

103 – A. length = 12, width = 4
Rationale: Use w to represent the width of the rectangle. The length is three times the width, so the length is 3w. The area of the rectangle is the length times the width, so the area is $w \cdot 3w$, or $3w^2$.

$3w^2 = 48$

Divide both sides of the equation by 3. You get:

$w^2 = 16$

So the width of the rectangle is 4 and the length of the rectangle is 12. Answer A is the correct choice.

104 – B. 10 miles
Rationale: If you made a simple map with these three cities, it would look like this:

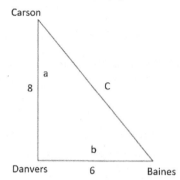

This is a right triangle. The longest side of a right triangle is called the hypotenuse. The two legs of the triangle are labeled a and b. The hypotenuse is labeled c. You can find the length of the hypotenuse (the distance between Caron and Baines) by using this equation: a2 + b2 = c2

In this case, the equation would be:
82 + 62 = c2

or

64 + 36 = c2
100 = c2

To find c, find which number times itself equals 100? The answer is 10. Answer B is the correct choice.

105   – B. 3,024 cubic inches
Rationale: The formula for the volume of a rectangular solid is length x width x height. So the volume of this box is:

18 x 12 x 14 = 3,024 cubic inches

Answer B is the correct choice.

106 – B. 6.5 x 10^{-3}
Rationale: Make a list of the negative powers of 10:

10^{-2} = 1/100 = 0.01
10^{-3} = 1/1000 = 0.001
10^{-4} = 1/10000 = 0.0001
10^{-5} = 1/100000 = 0.00001

Now multiply each of these numbers by 6.5 to see which one gives you 0.0065. The decimal must be moved 3 places to the left from 6.5 to 0.0065. Answer B is the correct choice.

<u>107 – D. 6096</u>
Rationale: Twenty feet multiplied by twelve inches per foot multiplied by 25.4 millimeters per inch gives a value of 6096 millimeters. Answer D is the correct choice.

<u>108 – A. 9.7 millimeters</u>
Rationale: The square base that is 4 inches on a side has an area of 4•4•2.54•2.54 or about 103 square centimeters. One hundred cubic centimeters divided by 103 square centimeters is approximately 0.97 centimeters or about 9.7 millimeters. Answer A is the correct choice.

<u>109 – C. 6.1 cubic inches</u>
Rationale: One inch is 2.54 centimeters. To convert centimeters to inches, divide by 2.54. Since a cubic centimeter is a centimeter times itself 3 times, to convert we divide by 2.54 three times. 100/2.54/2.54/2.54 equals about 6.1 cubic inches. Answer C is the correct choice.
<u>110 – A. 0.00075 kg</u>
Rationale: Twenty-five milligrams multiplied by 30 capsules is 750 milligrams. Dividing by 1000 is .75 grams. Dividing by 1000 again gives the answer in kilograms.

Answer A is the correct choice.

WRITING PRACTICE TEST

1. Which of the following choices best completes this sentence?
When asked if the sleeping pill had _____him at all, the man replied that it had had no _____;
nonetheless, he realized that he _____not attempt to drive his car that evening.
   a) affected; effect; ought
   b) affected; effect; aught
   c) effected; affect; ought
   d) effected; affect; aught

2. Which sentence makes best use of grammatical conventions for clarity and concision?
   a) Hiking along the trail, the birds chirped loudly and interrupted our attempt at a peaceful nature
      walk.
   b) The birds chirped loudly, attempting to hike along the nature trail we were interrupted.
   c) Hiking along the trail, we were assailed by the chirping of birds, which made our nature walk
      hardly the peaceful exercise we had wanted.
   d) Along the nature trail, our walk was interrupted by loudly chirping birds in our attempt at a
      nature trail.

3. Which word from the following sentence is an adjective?
A really serious modern-day challenge is finding a way to consume real food in a world of overly processed
food products.
   a) really
   b) challenge
   c) consume
   d) processed

4. To improve sentence fluency, how could you state the information below in a single sentence?
My daughter was in a dance recital. I attended it with my husband. She received an award. We were very
proud.
   a) My daughter, who was in a dance recital, received an award, which made my husband and I, who
      were in attendance, very proud.
   b) My husband and I attended my daughter's dance recital and were very proud when she received
      an award.
   c) Attending our daughter's dance recital, my husband and I were very proud to see her receive an
      award.
   d) Dancing in a recital, my daughter received an award which my husband and I, who were there,
      very proud.

5. Which sentence is punctuated correctly?
   a) Since the concert ended very late I fell asleep in the backseat during the car ride home.
   b) Since the concert ended very late: I fell asleep in the backseat during the car ride home.
   c) Since the concert ended very late; I fell asleep in the backseat during the car ride home.
   d) Since the concert ended very late, I fell asleep in the backseat during the car ride home.

6. Which of the choices below best completes the following sentence? Negotiations with the enemy are never fun, but during times of war_____ a necessary evil.
- a) its
- b) it's
- c) their
- d) they're

7. Which of the verbs below best completes the following sentence?
The a cappela group _____ looking forward to performing for the entire student body at the graduation ceremony.
- a) is
- b) are
- c) was
- d) be

8. What kind of sentence is this? I can't believe her luck!
- a) Declarative
- b) Imperative
- c) Exclamatory
- d) Interrogative

9. Identify the error in this sentence:
Irregardless of the expense, it is absolutely imperative that all drivers have liability insurance to cover any personal injury that may be suffered during a motor vehicle accident.
- a) Irregardless
- b) Imperative
- c) Liability
- d) Suffered

10. Which of the following sentences is grammatically correct?
- a) Between you and me, I brang back less books from my dorm room than I needed to study for my exams.
- b) Between you and I, I brought back less books from my dorm room then I needed to study for my exams.
- c) Between you and me, I brought back fewer books from my dorm room than I needed to study for my exam.
- d) Between you and me, I brought back fewer books from my dorm room then I needed to study for my exams.

11. Choose from the answers to complete this sentence with the proper verb and antecedent agreement:
Neither of _____ _____able to finish our supper.
- a) we; were
- b) we; was
- c) us; were
- d) us; was

12. Which word in the following sentence is a noun? The library books are overdue.
    a) The
    b) library
    c) books
    d) overdue

13. Which of the following is a simple sentence?
    a) Mary and Samantha ran and skipped and hopped their way home from school every day.
    b) Mary liked to hop but Samantha preferred to skip.
    c) Mary loved coloring yet disliked when coloring was assigned for math homework.
    d) Samantha thought Mary was her best friend but she was mistaken.

14. Which of the following is NOT a simple sentence?
    a) Matthew and Thomas had been best friends since grade school.
    b) Matthew was tall and shy, and Thomas was short and talkative.
    c) Matthew liked to get Thomas to pass notes to the little red-haired girl in the back row of math class.
    d) Matthew and Thomas would tease Mary and Samantha on their way home from school every day.

15. Which of the following sentences is punctuated correctly?
    a) "Theres a bus coming so hurry up and cross the street!" yelled Bob to the old woman.
    b) "There's a bus coming, so hurry up and cross the street", yelled Bob, to the old woman.
    c) "Theres a bus coming, so hurry up and cross the street,"! yelled Bob to the old woman.
    d) "There's a bus coming, so hurry up and cross the street!" yelled Bob to the old woman.

16. Which of the following sentences is punctuated correctly?
    a) It's a long to-do list she left for us today: make beds, wash breakfast dishes, go grocery shopping, do laundry, cook dinner, and read the twins a bedtime story.
    b) Its a long to-do list she left for us today; make beds; wash breakfast dishes; go grocery shopping; do laundry; cook dinner; and read the twins a bedtime story.
    c) It's a long to-do list she left for us today: make beds; wash breakfast dishes; go grocery shopping; do laundry; cook dinner; and read the twins a bedtime story.
    d) Its a long to-do list she left for us today: make beds, wash breakfast dishes, go grocery shopping, do laundry, cook dinner, and read the twins a bedtime story.

17. Which of the following sentences is written in the first person?
    a) My room was a mess so my mom made me clean it before I was allowed to leave the house.
    b) Her room was a mess so she had to clean it before she left for the concert.
    c) You had better clean up your room before your mom comes home!
    d) Sandy is a slob and never cleans up her own room until her mom makes her.

18. Which sentence follows the rules for capitalization?
   a) My second grade Teacher's name was Mrs. Carmicheal.
   b) The Pope gave a very emotional address to the crowd after Easter Sunday mass.
   c) The president of France is meeting with President Obama later this week.
   d) My family spent our summer vacations at grandpa Joe's cabin in the Finger Lakes region.

19. The girl returning home after her curfew found the _____ up the stairs to her bedroom maddening as it seemed every step she took on the old staircase yielded a loud _____.
Which of the following completes the sentence above?
   a) clime; creak
   b) clime; creek
   c) climb; creek
   d) climb; creak

20. By this time next summer, _____ my college coursework. Which of the following correctly completes the sentence above?
   a) I did complete
   b) I completed
   c) I will complete
   d) I will have completed

21. Which of the following choices best completes this sentence?
The teacher nodded her _____ to the classroom _____ who was teaching a portion of the daily lesson for the first time.
   a) assent; aide
   b) assent; aid
   c) ascent; aide
   d) ascent; aid

22. Which of the following sentences is grammatically correct?
   a) No one has offered to let us use there home for the office's end-of-year picnic.
   b) No one have offered to let we use their home for the office's end-of-year picnic.
   c) No one has offered to let ourselves use their home for the office's end-of-year picnic.
   d) No one has offered to let us use their home for the office's end-of-year picnic.

23. Which choice most effectively combines the information in the following sentences? The tornado struck. It struck without warning. It caused damage.
The damage was extensive.
   a) Without warning, the extensively damaging tornado struck.
   b) Having struck without warning, the damage was extensive with the tornado.
   c) The tornado struck without warning and caused extensive damage.
   d) Extensively damaging, and without warning, struck the tornado.

24.   Which word in the sentence below is a verb?
       Carrying heavy boxes to the attic caused her to throw out her back.
       a) Carrying
       b) to
       c) caused
       d) out

25. Which choice below most effectively combines the information in the following sentences?
His lecture was boring. I thought it would never end. My eyelids were drooping. My feet were going numb.
       a) His never-ending lecture made my eyelids droop, and my feet were going numb.
       b) My eyelids drooping and my feet going numb, I thought his boring lecture would never end.
       c) His lecture was boring and would not end; it made my eyelids droop and my feet go numb.
       d) Never-ending, his boring lecture caused me to have droopy eyelids and for my feet to go numb.

26. Which choice below correctly completes this sentence?
       Comets_____balls of dust and ice,
       _____ leftover materials that
       _____ planets during the formation of
       _____ solar system.
       a) Comets is balls of dust and ice, comprised of leftover materials that were not becoming planets during the formation of its solar system.
       b) Comets are balls of dust and ice, comprising leftover materials that are not becoming planets during the formation of our solar system.
       c) Comets are balls of dust and ice, comprised of leftover materials that became planets during the formation of their solar system.
       d) Comets are balls of dust and ice, comprised of leftover materials that did not become planets during the formation of our solar system.

Questions 27-35 are based on the following passage about Penny Dreadfuls.

Victorian era Britain experienced social changes that resulted in increased literacy rates. With the rise of capitalism and industrialization, people began to spend more money on entertainment, contributing to the popularization of the novel. Improvements in printing resulted in the production of newspapers, as well as, Englands' more fully recognizing the singular concept of reading as a form of leisure; it was, of itself, a new industry. An increased capacity for travel via the invention of tracks, engines, and the coresponding railway distribution created both a market for cheap popular literature, and the ability for it to be circulated on a large scale.

The first penny serials were published in the 1830s to meet this demand. The serials were priced to be affordable to working-class readers, and were considerably cheaper than the serialized novels of authors such as Charles Dickens, which cost a shilling (twelve pennies) per part. Those who could not afford a penny a week, working class boys often formed clubs sharing the cost, passed the booklets, who were flimsy, from reader to reader. Other enterprising youngsters would collect a number of consecutive parts, then rent the volume out to friends.

The stories themselves were reprints, or sometimes rewrites, of gothic thrillers, as well as new stories about famous criminals. Other serials were thinly-disguised plagiarisms of popular contemporary literature. The penny dreadfuls were influential since they were in the words of one commentator the most alluring and low-priced form of escapist reading available to ordinary youth.

In reality, the serial novels were overdramatic and sensational, but generally harmless. If anything, the penny dreadfuls, although obviously not the most enlightening or inspiring of literary selections, resulted in increasingly literate youth in the Industrial period. The wide circulation of this sensationalist literature, however, contributed to an ever greater fear of crime in mid-Victorian Britain.

27. Which of the following is the correct punctuation for the following sentence from paragraph 1?
    a) NO CHANGE
    b) Improvements in printing resulted in the production of newspapers, as well as England's more fully recognizing the singular concept of reading as a form of leisure; it was, of itself, a new industry.
    c) Improvements in printing resulted in the production of newspapers, as well as Englands more fully recognizing the singular concept of reading as a form of leisure; it was, of itself, a new industry.
    d) Improvements in printing resulted in the production of newspapers as well as, England's more fully recognizing the singular concept of reading as a form of leisure; it was, of itself, a new industry.

28. In the first sentence of paragraph 1, which of the following words should be capitalized?
    a) era
    b) social
    c) literacy
    d) rates

29. In the last sentence of paragraph 1, which of the following words is misspelled?
    a) capacity
    b) via
    c) coresponding
    d) cheap

30. In the first sentence of the paragraph 2, "this demand" refers to which of the following antecedents in paragraph 1?
    a) travel
    b) leisure
    c) industry
    d) market

31. Which of the following sentences is the clearest way to express the ideas in the third sentence of paragraph 2?
    a) A penny a week, working class boys could not afford these books; they often formed sharing clubs that were passing the flimsy booklets around from one reader to another reader.
    b) Clubs were formed to buy the flimsy booklets by working class boys who could not afford a penny a week that would share the cost, passing from reader to reader the flimsy booklets.
    c) Working class boys who could not afford a penny a week often formed clubs that would share the cost, passing the flimsy booklets from reader to reader.
    d) Sharing the cost were working class boys who could not afford a penny a week; they often formed clubs and, reader to reader, passed the flimsy booklets around.

32. Which word in the first sentence of paragraph 3 should be capitalized?
    a) stories
    b) gothic
    c) thrillers
    d) criminals

33. Which of the following versions of the final sentence of paragraph 3 is correctly punctuated?
    a) The penny dreadfuls were influential since they were in the words of one commentator; the most alluring and low-priced form of escapist reading available to ordinary youth.
    b) The penny dreadfuls were influential since they were, in the words of one commentator, "the most alluring and low-priced form of escapist reading available to ordinary youth".
    c) The penny dreadfuls were influential since they were, in the words of one commentator, the most alluring and low-priced form of escapist reading available to ordinary youth.
    d) The penny dreadfuls were influential since they were in the words of one commentator "the most alluring and low-priced form of escapist reading available to ordinary youth."

34. In this first sentence of paragraph, which of the following words is a noun?
    a) serial
    b) novels
    c) sensational
    d) generally

35. In the last sentence of paragraph, which of the following words is an adjective?
  a) circulation
  b) literature
  c) however
  d) greater

36. The author wants to add a sentence to the passage that would list some of the books which were plagiarized into penny dreadfuls. Which paragraph would be the best place to add this information?
  a) Paragraph 1
  b) Paragraph 2
  c) Paragraph 3
  d) Paragraph 4

Questions 37-43 are based on the following passage about Martin Luther King Jr.

Martin Luther King Jr. was an American baptist minister and activist who was a leader in the African-American Civil Rights Movement. He is best known for his role in the advancement of civil rights using non-violent civil disobedience based on his Christian beliefs. In the United States, his racial equality efforts, and his staunchly advocating civil rights is among, undoubtedly, culturally the most important contributions made by King to last century's society.

King became a civil rights activist early in his career. In 1955, he led the Montgomery bus boycott, and in 1957 he helped found the Southern Christian Leadership Conference (SCLC), serving as its first president. With the SCLC, King led an unsuccessful 1962 struggle against segregation in Albany, Georgia, and helped organize the 1963 nonviolent protests in Birmingham, Alabama. King also helped to organize the 1963 March on Washington where he delivered his famous I Have a Dream speech. There, he established his reputation as the greatest orator in American history.

On October 14, 1964, King justly received the Nobel Piece Prize for combating racial inequality through nonviolent resistance. In 1965, he helped to organize the famous Selma to Montgomery marches, and the following year he and SCLC took the movement north to Chicago to work on eliminating the unjust and much-despised segregated housing there. In the final years of his life, King expanded his focus to include opposition towards poverty and the Vietnam War, and he gave a famous speech in 1967 entitled "Beyond Vietnam". This speech alienated many of his liberal allies in government who supported the war, but to his credit King never allowed politics to dictate the path of his noble works.

In 1968, King was planning a national occupation of Washington, D.C., to be called the Poor People's Campaign, when he was assassinated on April 4 in Memphis, Tennessee. His violent death was, not surprisingly, followed by riots in many U.S. cities.

King was posthumously awarded the Presidential Medal of Freedom and the Congressional Gold Metal. Martin Luther King, Jr. Day was established as a holiday in numerous cities and states beginning in 1971, and eventually became a U.S. federal holiday in 1986. Since his tragic death, numerous streets in the U.S. have been renamed in his honor, and a county in Washington State was also renamed for him. The Martin Luther King, Jr. Memorial on the National Mall in Washington, D.C., was dedicated in 2011.

37. In the first sentence of paragraph 1, which of the following words should be capitalized?
   a) baptist
   b) minister
   c) activist
   d) leader

38. Which is the best rewording for clarity and concision of this sentence from paragraph 1?
   a) His efforts to achieve racial equality in the United States, and his staunch public advocacy of civil rights are undoubtedly among the most important cultural contributions made to society in the last century.
   b) His efforts achieving equality in the United States, and to staunchly advocate civil rights are undoubtedly among the most important contributions culturally and societally made in the last century.
   c) Racial equality and civil rights, staunchly advocated by King in the United States, are, without a doubt, last century's greatest contributions, in a cultural way, to society.
   d) Last century, King made cultural contributions to racial equality and civil rights, which are undoubtedly the greatest made in the previous century.

39. Which of the following found in paragraph 2 should be placed inside quotation marks?
   a) Montgomery bus boycott
   b) Southern Christian Leadership Conference
   c) March on Washington
   d) I Have a Dream

40. In the first sentence of paragraph 3, which of the following words is misspelled?
   a) received
   b) Piece
   c) combating
   d) racial

41. In the first sentence of paragraph 5, which of the following words is misspelled?
   a) Posthumously
   b) Presidential
   c) Medal
   d) Metal

42. Which of the following sentences from the passage provides context clues about the author's feelings in regard to King?
   a) He is best known for his role in the advancement of civil rights using non-violent civil disobedience based on his Christian beliefs. (P. 1)
   b) King also helped to organize the 1963 March on Washington where he delivered his famous I Have a Dream speech. (P. 2)
   c) This speech alienated many of his liberal allies in government who supported the war, but to his credit King never allowed politics to dictate the path of his noble works. (P. 3)
   d) King was posthumously awarded the Presidential Medal of Freedom and the Congressional Gold Metal. (P. 5)

43. The author is considering adding a paragraph about King's family to the passage. Should he or she do this?
- a) Yes, because it adds needed personal details to the passage.
- b) Yes, because it would elaborate on information already provided in the passage.
- c) No, because the passage is about King's public life and works, and information about his family would be irrelevant.
- d) No, because information about his family has already been included and an additional paragraph on that topic would be redundant.

44. Which of the following sentences uses correct punctuation for dialogue?
- a) "Hey, can you come here a second"? asked Marie.
- b) She thought about his offer briefly and then responded. "I think I will have to pass".
- c) "I am making pancakes for breakfast. Does anybody want some?" asked mom.
- d) The conductor yelled "All aboard"! and then waited for last minute travelers to board the train.

45. Which of the following is a compound sentence?
- a) She and I drove to the play together.
- b) I woke up early that morning and began to do long-neglected household chores.
- c) The long-separated cousins ran and jumped and sang and played all afternoon.
- d) I trembled when I saw him: his face was white as a ghost.

46. Which of the following is the best order for the sentences below in forming a logical paragraph?
- a) A, B, C, D, E
- b) A, C, E, B, D
- c) A, D, B, D, E
- d) A, C, E, D, B

A. Walt Disney was a shy, self-deprecating and insecure man in private but adopted a warm and outgoing public persona.

B. His film work continues to be shown and adapted; his studio maintains high standards in its production of popular entertainment, and the Disney amusement parks have grown in size and number to attract visitors in several countries.

C. However he had high standards and high expectations of those with whom he worked.

D. He nevertheless remains an important figure in the history of animation and in the cultural history of the United States, where he is considered a national cultural icon.

E. His reputation changed in the years after his death, from a purveyor of homely patriotic values to a representative of American imperialism.

47. Which of the choices below is the meaning of the word "adopted" in the following sentence? *Walt Disney was a shy, self-deprecating and insecure man in private but adopted a warm and outgoing public persona.*
- a) took
- b) began to use
- c) began to have
- d) legally cared for as one's own child

48. Which of the following sentences is written in the second person?
    a) You had better call and RSVP to the party right away before you forget.
    b) She had every intention of calling with a prompt reply to the invitation, but the week got hectic and she forgot.
    c) I am utterly hopeless at remembering things, so I will set up a calendar reminder for myself to call Jan about the party.
    d) "Did you forget to RSVP to the party?!" asked her exasperated roommate.

49. Which of the following sentences shows proper pronoun-antecedent agreement?
    a) The author published several best-selling novels; some of it was made into films that were not as popular.
    b) Everyone should bring their parents to the town-wide carnival.
    c) Smart companies will do what it takes to hold onto its best employees.
    d) Parents are reminded to pick up their children from school promptly at 2:30.

50. Which of the following sentences shows proper subject-verb agreement?
    a) Danny is one of the only students who have lived up to his responsibilities as a newspaper staff member.
    b) One of my friends are going to be on a TV series starting this fall.
    c) Rice and beans, my favorite meal, reminds me of my native country Puerto Rico.
    d) Most of the milk we bought for the senior citizens' luncheons have gone bad.

51. Which sentence below illustrates proper use of punctuation for dialogue?
    a) "I have a dream", began Martin Luther King, Jr.
    b) "Can you believe that I have been asked to audition for that part," asked Megan excitedly?
    c) "You barely know him! How can she marry him?" was the worried mother's response at her teenager's announcement of marriage.
    d) "Remain seated while the seatbelt signs are illuminated." Came the announcement over the airplane's loud speaker system.

52. Which of the sentences below is NOT in the second person?
    a) "I have a dream", began Martin Luther King, Jr.
    b) "Can you believe that I have been asked to audition for that part," asked Megan excitedly?
    c) "You barely know him! How can you marry him?" was the worried mother's response at her teenager's announcement of marriage.
    d) "Remain seated while the seatbelt signs are illuminated." Came the announcement over the airplane's loud speaker system.

53. Which of the following sentences is an example of an Imperative sentence?
    a) "I have a dream", began Martin Luther King, Jr.
    b) "Can you believe that I have been asked to audition for that part," asked Megan excitedly?
    c) "You barely know him! How can she marry him?" was the worried mother's response at her teenager's announcement of marriage.
    d) "Please remain seated while the seatbelt signs are illuminated." Came the announcement over the airplane's loud speaker system.

54. Which of the following means "the act of cutting out"?
    a) Incision
    b) Concision
    c) Excision
    d) Decision

55. Which of the following refers to an inflammation?
    a) Appendectomy
    b) Colitis
    c) Angioplasty
    d) Dermatology

56. Which of the following refers to a cancer?
    a) Neuropathy
    b) Hysterectomy
    c) Oncology
    d) Melanoma

57. Which of the following conditions is associated with the nose?
    a) Hematoma
    b) Neuralgia
    c) Rhinitis
    d) Meningitis

58. Which of the following refers to the study of something?
    a) Gastroenterology
    b) Gastritis
    c) Psychosis
    d) Psychopath

Writing Practice Test – Answer Key

1.   A. affected; effect; ought
Rationale: Since a verb is needed in the first blank, "affected" not "effected" (a noun) will work; but the noun "effect" is correct in the second blank. "ought", meaning "should" correctly completes the sentence, indicating he should not drive. "aught", meaning zero, or nothing, or none, does not make sense in this context.

2.   C. Hiking along the trail, we were assailed by the chirping of birds, which made our nature walk hardly the peaceful exercise we had wanted.
Rationale: Who was hiking along the trail? "we" were, so only option C works. The other options are dangling participles: in option b, the birds were not attempting to hike, so that doesn't make sense; in option a, again, the birds were hiking along the trail, so that makes no sense; option d is just poorly constructed and makes the meaning overall unclear.

3.   D. processed
Rationale: "Processed" modifies "food products" so that is the adjective; "really" is an adverb modifying the adjective "serious"; "challenge" is a noun, which is a person, place or thing; "consume" is a verb, a word that shows action.

4.   B. My husband and I attended my daughter's dance recital and were very proud when she received an award.
Rationale: The most clear and concise sentence is option b; all the information is included, it is presented logically, it flows smoothly off the tongue, and it is not overly wordy.

5.   D. Since the concert ended very late, I fell asleep in the backseat during the car ride home.
Rationale: Option d is correct. "Since the concert ended very late" is a dependent clause which explains why "I fell asleep..."; since they are dependent, the only proper way to link them is with a comma.

6.   D. they're
Rationale: This question asks you make pronoun and antecedent agree; in this sentence the antecedent is "negotiations"; since this is a plural noun, the pronoun must also be plural, but the blank is also missing a verb. The only option with a plural pronoun and a verb is the contraction "they're".

7.   A. is
Rationale: "Group", a singular noun, is the subject of the sentence, so a singular verb is needed. Also needed is a present tense helping verb for "looking forward". The only option that satisfies both is "is".

8.   C. Exclamatory
Rationale: An exclamatory sentence is a type of sentence that expresses strong feelings by making an exclamation. Therefore, the above sentence is an exclamatory sentence.

9.   A. Irregardless
Rationale: "Irregardless" is incorrect as it is a double-negative: the suffix "less" already indicates a lack of regard, so the addition of the negative "ir" before the correct word, regardless, is unnecessary.

10.   C. Between you and me, I brought back fewer books from my dorm room than I needed to study for my exam.
Rationale: C. "Brought" is the correct past tense form of bring; "fewer" is the correct word to describe an exact number of items, whereas "less" is used to refer to an amount of something that cannot be exactly counted, like sand or air or water; and "than" is the correct spelling of the word that shows a comparison between two things.

11.   D. us; was
Rationale: D. Words that follow prepositions are considered to be in the objective case, therefore "us" is the correct word here; "Neither", a single pronoun, is the subject of the sentence, so a singular verb, "was" is needed to properly complete it.

12.   C. books
Rationale: C. A noun is a person, place or thing. While a "library" is usually used as a noun to denote a place where people can go to borrow books, or look up information, in this sentence it is used as an adjective to modify "books", which is the only true noun in the sentence.

13.   A. Mary and Samantha ran and skipped and hopped their way home from school every day.
Rationale: A. A simple sentence is one which has one subject and one verb, though both the subject and verb can be compound. In this case, option a is a simple sentence, with the one subject being compound ("Mary and Samantha") and the one verb also being compound ("ran and skipped and hopped"). The other options either have more than one subject or more than one verb.

14.   B. Matthew was tall and shy, and Thomas was short and talkative.
Rationale: B. A simple sentence is one which has one subject and one verb, though both the subject and verb can be compound. Linked by the conjunction "and", sentence B is the only compound sentence above because it links the first sentence "Matthew was tall and shy" with the second sentence "Thomas was short and talkative".

15.   D. "There's a bus coming, so hurry up and cross the street!" yelled Bob to the old woman.
Rationale: D. "There's" is the subject and verb of the sentence written as a contraction so the apostrophe is needed; a comma is needed before "so" because what follows it is a dependent clause which must be separated from the single sentence with a comma. When writing dialogue, the punctuation is included inside the quotation marks; in this case an exclamation is appropriate because Bob is warning the old woman to get out of the way of the oncoming bus; the use of the verb "yelled" is a clue that the statement by Bob is exclamatory.

16.   C. It's a long to-do list she left for us today: make beds; wash breakfast dishes; go grocery shopping; do laundry; cook dinner; and read the twins a bedtime story.
Rationale: "It's" is the subject and verb joined together in a contraction, so an apostrophe is needed. The sentence introduces a list, so it must be preceded by a colon; because the list is comprised of phrases instead of single words, a semicolon is needed to separate each item.

17.   A. My room was a mess so my mom made me clean it before I was allowed to leave the house.
Rationale: The use of the possessive pronoun "my" and the singular pronoun "I" indicates that the sentence is written from the first person perspective. "You" and "your" are second person; "her" or "him" are third person.

18.   C. The president of France is meeting with President Obama later this week.
Rationale: C. When referring to the "president of France", "president" is just a noun denoting his position, so it is not capitalized. In the case of "President Obama", "President" is the title by which he is addressed, so it is a proper noun and requires capitalization. The other options are incorrectly capitalized.

19.   D. climb; creak
Rationale: "Climb" is the proper spelling to denote ascending the stairs; "clime" refers to climate. "Creak" denotes a squeaky sound; "creek" denotes a stream or small moving waterway.

20.   D. I will have completed
Rationale: D. The FUTURE PERFECT TENSE indicates that an action will have been finished at some point in the future. This tense is formed with "will" plus "have" plus the past participle of the verb (which can be either regular or irregular in form). "By this time next summer" is the clue that lets you know the coursework will be done some time in the future.

21.   A. assent; aide
Rationale: A. The word "Assent" means approval, which is what the teacher wants to do to show encouragement to novice teacher who is currently her "aide" or assistance in the classroom. "Ascent" denotes a climb; "aid" is a verb denoting the action of helping.

22.   D. No one has offered to let us use their home for the office's end-of-year picnic.
Rationale: D. "No one", a singular pronoun, requires a singular verb, "has". "Us" is the objective case pronoun which is needed to follow the verb "to let"; "ourselves" is the reflexive case which is not needed in this sentence; "we" is subjective. "Their" shows possession of "home"; spelled "there", this word denotes location (e.g. here or there).

23.   C. The tornado struck without warning and caused extensive damage.
Rationale: C. Incorporating all of the information from the four sentences logically and concisely, option C is the best choice.

24.   C. caused
Rationale: C. "Caused" is the verb in this sentence; "Carrying" is the subject. Though it may look like a verb, it is actually a gerund (a verb acting as a noun) which is the subject. Deleting extraneous words will help see this, so let's rewrite the sentence in its most basic form: "Carrying caused her to throw out her back." This way it is clear to see that "carrying" is the subject, and is not a verb.

25.   B. My eyelids drooping and my feet going numb, I thought his boring lecture would never end.
Rationale: B. This sentence most clearly concisely conveys all of the information in the four above sentences; structure is parallel and no awkward or extraneous words are included.

26.   D. Comets are balls of dust and ice, comprised of leftover materials that did not become planets during the formation of our solar system.
Rationale: D. "Comets" (a plural subject requiring a plural verb) "are" "comprised of" (meaning: made up of) leftover materials that "did not" (in the past) become planets during the formation of "our" solar system.

27.   B. Improvements in printing resulted in the production of newspapers, as well as England's more fully recognizing the singular concept of reading as a form of leisure; it was, of itself, a new industry.
Rationale: B. The sentence is a compound sentence (two complete subject and verb phrases), so these should be separated by a comma after newspapers. The possession of recognition of the singular concept of reading by England needs to be shown with an apostrophe plus "s": "England's".

28.   A. era
Rationale: A. The Victorian Era is a two-word proper noun referring to a time period in history so "era" should be capitalized. The other words should not be capitalized.

29.   C. coresponding
Rationale: C. The correct spelling is corresponding.

30.   D. market
Rationale: D. "this demand" refers back to the "market (for cheaper literature)" in the last sentence of paragraph 2.

31.   C. Working class boys who could not afford a penny a week often formed clubs that would share the cost, passing the flimsy booklets from reader to reader.
Rationale: C. This sentence most clearly and concisely expresses the idea of book sharing amongst working boys who could not afford to spend a penny every week to buy the penny dreadfuls.

32.   B. gothic
Rationale: B. The word Gothic is a proper adjective referring to a specific genre of literature. None of the other words in this sentence should be capitalized.

33.   D. The penny dreadfuls were influential since they were in the words of one commentator "the most alluring and low-priced form of escapist reading available to ordinary youth."
Rationale: D. The independent clause "in the words of one commentator" needs to be set off by commas on either end; and since it is a direct quote, the last part of the sentence needs to be in quotation marks. The period at the end of the sentence needs to be inside the quotation marks.

34.   B. novels
Rationale: B. A noun is a person, place or thing. "Novels" is a plural noun which denotes a thing that can be read. "Serial" and "sensational" are adjectives; "generally" is an adverb.

35.   D. greater
Rationale: D. An adjective is a word which describes a noun. In this sentence, "greater" is an adjective describing fear. "Circulation" and "literature" are nouns; "however" is a pronoun.

36.   C. Paragraph 3
Rationale: C. Paragraph mentions that penny dreadfuls were often plagiarized versions of other popular literature at the time, so this would be the best place to add a sentence of supporting detail about this.

37.   A. baptist
Rationale: A. As the word identifies King's religion, "Baptist" should be capitalized.

38.   A. His efforts to achieve racial equality in the United States, and his staunch public advocacy of civil rights are undoubtedly among the most important cultural contributions made to society in the last century.
Rationale: A. Using parallel structure and no extraneous verbiage, option A is the most clear and concise of the versions.

39.   D. I Have a Dream
Rationale: D. "I Have a Dream" is the title of a speech and should therefore be put inside quotation marks.

40.   B. Piece
Rationale: B. In this sentence, "Piece" should be spelled Peace, as in harmony or an absence of fighting.

41.   D. Metal
Rationale: D. In this sentence, "Metal" should be spelled "Medal", as an award or honor, not "metal" as in a naturally occurring element or raw material.

42.   C. This speech alienated many of his liberal allies in government who supported the war, but to his credit King never allowed politics to dictate the path of his noble works. (P. 3)
Rationale: C. The phrase "to his credit" and the description of his works as "noble" provide clues that the author has a positive perspective about Martin Luther King and the role his activism played in American history.

43.   C. No, because the passage is about King's public life and works, and information about his family would be irrelevant.
Rationale: C. The focus of the passage is about King's work as a minister and activist, so details about his family are unrelated to this focus, and therefore should be left out.

44.   C. "I am making pancakes for breakfast. Does anybody want some?" asked mom.
Rationale: Only option C correctly includes sentence punctuation for quoted statements: punctuation for dialogue should be inside quotation marks, as is illustrated with mom asking if anyone wants pancakes; the question mark is within the quotation marks.

45.   B. I woke up early that morning and began to do long-neglected household chores.
Rationale: Option B contains two simple sentences, which when combined make a compound sentence:" I woke up early than morning" AND "I began to do long-neglected household chores."

46.   D. A, C, E, D, B
Rationale: D. The most logical progression of ideas is in option D. The topic of Disney's public persona is introduced, and is then contrasted with his treatment of people at work, and then the transformation of his persona from that of an American patriot to an imperialist. Finally, the paragraph is wrapped up with statements about the importance of his work and his current legacy in popular culture.

47.   C. began to have
Rationale: C. The sentence is discussing the contrast between Disney's private and public personas, stating that he began to have a public persona which was very different than the way he was in private.

48.   A. You had better call and RSVP to the party right away before you forget.
Rationale: A. Statements which show direct address, and use the pronoun "you" are referred to as the second person. Though the exclamation uses the pronoun you, it is a quoted statement, so it is really in the third person. Only choice A is an example of second person writing.

49.   D. Parents are reminded to pick up their children from school promptly at 2:30.
Rationale: D. Only D makes proper use of pronouns and their antecedents: in A, novels and it do not agree; in B, everyone is singular, so instead of their, the pronoun should be him or her; in C, companies and it do not agree.

50.   C. Rice and beans, my favorite meal, reminds me of my native country Puerto Rico.
Rationale: Choice C is the only sentence in which subject (rice and beans/meal) and verb (reminds) agree: in A, one and have lived do not agree; in B, one and are going do not agree; and in D, most (of the milk OR it) does not agree with have gone.

51.　　C. "You barely know him! How can she marry him?" was the worried mother's response at her teenager's announcement of marriage.
Rationale: C. Sentence punctuation always is inside quotation marks; therefore, option C is punctuated correctly for dialogue.

52.　　A. "I have a dream", began Martin Luther King, Jr.
Rationale: A. Second person uses the pronoun "you" or features direct address. Though punctuated incorrectly, it is clear that only the first sentence is not written in the second person; the use of "I" illustrates first person.

53.　　D. "Please remain seated while the seatbelt signs are illuminated." Came the announcement over the airplane's loud speaker system.
Rationale: D. An Imperative statement is one which gives a command. Though punctuated incorrectly, it is clear that option D is imperative: the announcement is commanding the passengers to remain seated.

54.　　C. Excision
Rationale: C. The prefix "ex" means out, so that is our clue here. "Excision" refers to a surgical procedure done to cut out something unwanted or unnecessary.

55.　　B – Colitis
Rationale: B. The suffix "itis" is one which refers to inflammation, so "colitis" is an inflammation of the colon.

56.　　D. Melanoma
Rationale: The suffix "oma" refers to a tumor or cancer, so "melanoma" refers to a cancer of the skin (coming from melanin, that which gives our skin its color). "Oncology" is the study of cancer, but it does not refer to cancer itself.

57.　　C. Rhinitis
Rationale: The root "rhino" refers to the nose or nasal area, so "rhinitis" is an inflammation of the nasal passages.

58.　　A. Gastroenterology
Rationale: A. The suffix "logy" refers to the study of some discipline or area, therefore gastroenterology is the study or examination of the gastrointestinal area of the body.

Made in United States
Orlando, FL
20 March 2025

59672081R00079